MOVE IT!

STUDENTS' BOOK

KATHERINE STANNETT AND FIONA BEDDALL

SERIES CONSULTANT: CARA NORRIS-RAMIREZ

Starter Unit

Grammar and Vocabulary

• *To be* and *have*

1 Complete the text with the correct form of *be* or *have*.

Hi. My name [1] *is* James, and I [2] .... sixteen. I [3] .... a new MP3 player. It [4] .... red. It [5] .... a thousand songs on it, but it [6] .... (not) any rap songs because rap music [7] .... (not) my thing. [8] .... (you) an MP3 player? What [9] .... your favorite songs?

• Daily routines

2 Complete the phrases (1–9) with these words. Then match them to the pictures (a–i).

bus	dishes	do	~~dressed~~	make
school	take	teeth	walk	

1 get *dressed*
2 .... the dog
3 take the ....
4 .... your bed
5 do the ....
6 .... a shower
7 drive to ....
8 .... your homework
9 brush your ....

3 Which things from Exercise 2 do you do every day? What other things do you do every day?

• Present simple

4 Make sentences and questions. Use the Present simple.

1 Where / you / live / ? *Where do you live?*
2 She / not study / geography
3 He / take a shower / every morning
4 They / drive / to the supermarket / ?
No / they. They / take / the bus
5 I / not walk / the dog / every day
6 What / she / want / for dinner?
7 He / never / watch / TV
8 She / always / do / the dishes

• Present continuous

5 Complete the phone conversation with the Present continuous form of the verbs.

A [1] *Are you having* (you/have) a good morning?
B No, I [2] .... . I [3] .... (wait) for Lucy and Grace, and I [4] .... (get) bored.
A Why [5] .... (you/wait) for them?
B My mom [6] .... (not/work) today, so we [7] .... (plan) a trip to a theme park. But Lucy and Grace [8] .... (travel) to my house by bus right now, and it's the slowest bus in history!

• Present simple and continuous

6 Choose the correct words.

1 I *make* / *am making* my bed at 8 o'clock every morning.
2 Where *do you go* / *are you going* now?
3 His mother is from Mexico, so she *speaks* / *is speaking* Spanish at home.
4 We never *get* / *are getting* dressed before breakfast.
5 They *stay* / *are staying* with their grandparents at the moment.
6 I *love* / *am loving* science fiction stories.
7 *Does it rain* / *Is it raining* a lot in spring?
8 He *doesn't study* / *isn't studying* French this year.

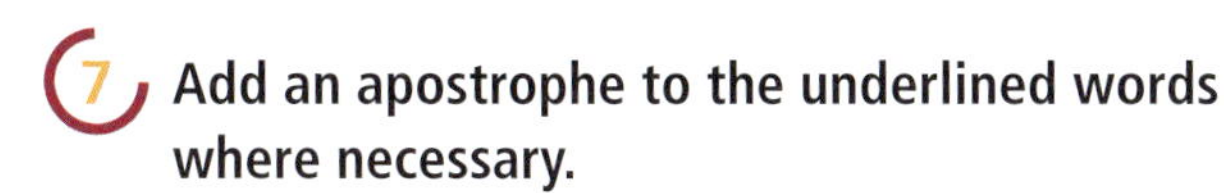

Apostrophes

7 Add an apostrophe to the underlined words where necessary.

Charlie has three brothers. His two younger brothers names are Jack and Will, and his oldest brothers Fred. Freds an actor. He isnt in any famous movies, but he has a part in a musical called *Billy Elliot*. It tells the story of a boy whos trying to become a dancer. The boys dad doesnt want a dancer in the family, but his dance teacher helps him. Its a really good show.

Pronouns and possessive adjectives

8 Choose the correct options.

1 Please help *me* / *my*.
2 *He* / *Him* is my best friend.
3 It isn't yours; it's *our* / *ours*.
4 What's *him* / *his* name?
5 What a big dog! Look at *it's* / *its* teeth.
6 Come and see *us* / *our* next week.
7 They want a cell phone like *mine* / *my*.
8 Do you like *they* / *them*?
9 I can't see *you* / *your*.

Useful adjectives

9 Complete the sentences with these words.

awesome	beautiful	~~colorful~~	dirty	disgusting
huge	popular	quiet	sore	tiny

1 Her clothes are very *colorful*. She loves wearing orange and purple.
2 I live in a .... village. There are no noisy streets here.
3 Basketball is a very .... sport for boys in the US. Almost everyone plays it.
4 She's .... at math. She never gets a wrong answer!
5 My boots are .... . I must clean them.
6 This food is .... . I can't eat it.
7 Go and see the doctor about your .... throat.
8 An elephant is a .... animal.
9 A chihuahua is a .... type of dog, usually only 15 cm tall.
10 It's a .... , sunny day.

Comparatives and superlatives

10 Complete the sentences with these words. Use comparatives or superlatives.

clothes	Danny Dream's	guitar	hair
Little Luke	music	Robbie T	~~singer~~

1 Danny Dream is the *worst singer*. (bad)
2 Danny Dream is .... than .... . (tall)
3 Robbie T has the .... . (short)
4 Danny Dream is .... than .... . (popular)
5 Robbie T is wearing the .... . (colorful)
6 Robbie T's guitar is .... than .... guitar. (big)
7 Danny Dream has the .... . (tiny)
8 Robbie T plays the .... . (quiet)

11 Make six sentences about people you know with the comparative or superlative of these adjectives.

annoying	bad	cool	famous	good	thin

• Free-time activities

12 Match 1–8 to a–h. Then match the activities to the pictures.

1 play *d*	a surfing
2 listen	b gymnastics
3 use	c text messages
4 send	d the saxophone *picture g*
5 go	e to rap music
6 do	f basketball
7 play	g a horror movie
8 watch	h the Internet

13 Copy and complete the table with these words.

classical comedy ~~drums~~ fantasy horror ice hockey judo keyboard reggae rock skiing swimming tennis ~~track~~ violin

Sports with *do*	Sports with *go*	Sports with *play*
track	....	....
Musical instruments	**Types of movies**	**Types of music**
drums	....	....

• Relative pronouns

14 Complete the sentences with *who, which* or *where*.

1 That's the girl *who* lives next to my uncle.
2 A bank is a place .... you can get cash.
3 Which is the classroom .... Ms. Tucker teaches?
4 Is that the coat .... you're borrowing from Sam?
5 This is the hospital .... my dad works.
6 I like the sausages .... they sell at the market.
7 He's the actor .... is in that historical movie.
8 They're the kids .... I see every day on the bus.

15 Make true sentences. Use the words in the table. Then write three more sentences with *who, which* or *where* and your own ideas.

1 school	place	who	you put on the floor
2 journalist	thing	which	buys things
3 rug	person	where	you can stay
4 customer			children learn
5 hotel			goes on top of a bed
6 comforter			reports the news

1 *A school is a place where children learn.*

• *Some* and *any*

16 Complete the sentences with *some* or *any*.

1 Do you have *any* money?
2 There aren't .... movie theaters in my town.
3 I have .... apples. Would you like one?
4 There's .... water in the plastic bottle.
5 We don't have .... homework tonight.
6 Are there .... fish in the lake?

• *Much, many* and *a lot of*

17 Choose the correct words.

1 She has *much* / *a lot of* nice clothes.
2 How *much* / *many* time is there before our next class?
3 We need *much* / *a lot of* volunteers to help us.
4 There aren't *much* / *many* people here.
5 Do they have *much* / *many* DVDs?
6 You're making too *much* / *a lot of* noise.
7 How *much* / *many* magazines do you read?
8 We have too *much* / *many* problems with our computer.

• Feelings adjectives

18 Complete the words.

1 I'm ex*cite*d about our vacation next week.
2 They're feeling pretty rel _ x _ _ about the test.
3 I'm af _ _ _ d of snakes.
4 He gets really a _ _ ry when you're rude.
5 They're b _ _ _ d of rice for dinner every day.
6 I'm so e _ b _ r _ _ _ s _ d about my terrible dancing last night!
7 She's u _ _ et about her brother's accident.
8 You're j _ _ l _ _ s of her because she's pretty.
9 I'm n _ _ v _ _ s about the game. It's really important that we win it.
10 She feels l _ _ _ ly without her friends.
11 She's p _ _ _ d of her good grade on the exam.
12 I'm t _ _ ed of baseball. Let's play a different sport.

• Past simple

19 Complete the conversation. Use the Past simple form of *be*.

A There [1] *were* some good shows on TV last night.
B Really? I [2] .... (not) at home. I [3] .... at Meg's house.
A Why [4] .... (you) there?
B She [5] .... upset about her exams.
A What [6] .... the problem?
B Her grades [7] ... (not) very good, and her parents [8] .... angry with her.
A [9] .... (she) happier after your visit?
B Yes, she [10] .... .

20 Complete the sentences with the Past simple form of the verbs.

1 We *watched* (watch) an action movie last night.
2 They .... (seem) very happy at Katie's house.
3 I .... (argue) with Simon yesterday.
4 They .... (travel) to the island by boat.
5 She .... (study) glaciers in geography last year.

21 Make the sentences in Exercise 20 negative.

1 *We didn't watch an action movie last night.*

22 Make Past simple questions and answers.

1 you / like / the movie? ✗
Did you like the movie? No, I didn't.
2 they / talk / to Katie's mom ✓
3 you and Simon / argue / about the project? ✓
4 they / get / to the island / by plane? ✗
5 she / study / with Mr. Davis? ✓

• Irregular verbs

23 Read about Connor's exciting day. Copy and complete the table with the verbs in bold.

Infinitive	Past simple
buy	*bought*

1

2

3

4

5

6

1 In the morning he **bought** some sneakers. His friend Jake **sold** them to him.
2 Then he **ate** a banana and **drank** some juice.
3 Later he **ran** in a race and **won**.
4 After the race, the organizers **spoke** to him and **gave** him a prize.
5 He **wrote** a text message and **sent** it to all his family and friends.
6 His parents **heard** the news and **felt** proud.

• Telling the time

24 Match these times to the clocks in the pictures in Exercise 23.

a three forty-five *4*
b three thirty
c two o'clock
d five past four
e ten to four
f eleven fifteen

25 What did you do yesterday? At what time? Write six sentences.

At eight fifteen I went to school.

Speaking and Listening

1 1.2 **Read and listen to the conversation. Answer the questions.**

1 Is Holly happy or sad?
2 Why does she feel this way?

2 **Copy and complete the table.**

Name	*Yasmin*
Appearance	....
Character	....
Hobbies/Interests	....

3 **Act out the conversation in groups of three.**

4 **Complete the questions. Match them to the answers.**

1 *How* are you? *b*
2 What's she .... ?
3 Is she interested .... soccer?

a No, she isn't.
b Fine, thanks.
c She's really confident.

Fraser Hey, Holly! How are you?
Holly Fine, thanks. Better than fine, in fact. I have some really good news. My cousin Yasmin is moving to Concord soon, and she's going to go to our school!
Archie Was she the girl with long dark hair who stayed with you last summer?
Holly That's right. Look, I have a photo of her on my phone.
Fraser What's she like?
Holly She's really confident … and very talkative.
Archie I remember that. She talked and talked!
Holly Well, she has a lot of interesting things to talk about.
Fraser Is she interested in soccer?
Holly No, she isn't, but she does a lot of dancing in her free time. She loves fashion and hip hop music, too. I think you'll like her.
Archie Yes, she seemed really nice last year.

Unread Message

From holly:)brightman@my_mail

Subject Moving to Concord!

Hi Yasmin,

I'm so excited that you're moving to Concord. We'll be neighbors!

I hope you will like it here. It's a small town, but a lot of nice people live here. My best friends, Fraser and Archie, live on my street. Archie's the boy who you met last summer. Do you remember him? He's tall like me, and he has short dark hair. He's really good fun. He's sometimes a little selfish, but I don't mind. I can be selfish, too! You didn't meet Fraser, but you'll like him. He has blond hair like me. He's shy, but he's very generous. He's smart, so you can ask him for help with your homework.

There are only 700 students at Concord High, our school, so it's smaller than your school in Philadelphia. Some of the teachers give too much homework, but everyone's really friendly. There are a lot of after-school activities, and they're a good way to make new friends. Archie and I do judo after school, and Fraser plays soccer. We're all in a drama club, too. There's also a dance club. I'll try to find out more about it for you.

I'm sending a photo of you in the clothes that you bought when we went shopping. You look so cool!

Lots of love,

Holly

SEND

Reading

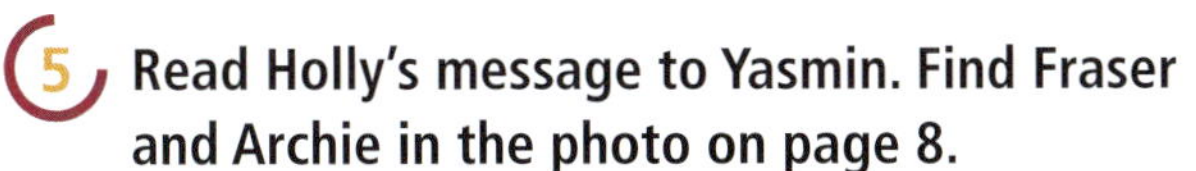
5 Read Holly's message to Yasmin. Find Fraser and Archie in the photo on page 8.

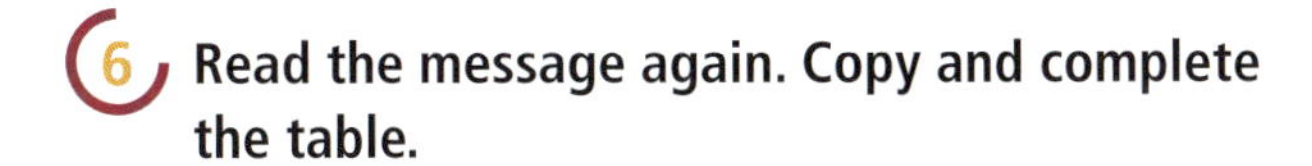
6 Read the message again. Copy and complete the table.

Name	Holly	Archie	Fraser
Appearance	*tall, blond hair*	....	....
Character	....	....	....
Hobbies/ Interests	....	....	....

Writing

7 Copy and complete the table about a friend of yours. Then write a paragraph about him/her.

Name	
Appearance	
Character	
Hobbies/Interests	

My assessment profile: Workbook page 126

1 Different Lives

Grammar
Past simple vs
Past continuous; *used to* for past habits

Vocabulary
Compound nouns;
Phrasal verbs 1

Speaking
Expressing extremes

Writing
Telling a story

Word list page 43
Workbook page 104

Vocabulary • Compound nouns

1 **Match these words to the correct headings. Copy and complete the table.**
1.3 **Then listen, check and repeat.**

~~babysitter~~	business person	classmate	firefighter	homework
lighthouse	skyscraper	snowmobile	spaceship	speedboat
whiteboard	windmill			

jobs	*babysitter*	....	....
transportation	....	....	....
school	....	....	....
building	....	....	....

2 **Match the words in Exercise 1 to the pictures.**

babysitter *10*

3 **Match the clues to the correct words in Exercise 1.**

1 This sends a light out across the ocean. *lighthouse*
2 This person works in an office and wears dress clothes.
3 This person stops buildings from burning down.
4 You can make flour in this building.
5 A teacher uses this in class.
6 You can travel fast in this when it's very cold.
7 Some people believe that aliens travel in this.
8 You use this on the water.
9 You are probably sitting next to one now!
10 You do this after school.
11 Most big cities have these. They are very tall.
12 This person takes care of very young children.

1.4 **Pronunciation Unit 1** page 121

Brain Trainer Unit 1
Activities 1 and 2
Go to page 112

Reading

1 **Read the article quickly. Match the people (1–3) to the photos (a–c).**

2 **Read the article again. Answer the questions.**

1.5

1 Who was helping his/her family? *Flora and Tom*
2 Who uses a phone?
3 Who spent a long time at school?
4 Who was studying?
5 Who works in the summer?

3 **In pairs, ask and answer.**

1 Whose life is most like yours?
2 Which facts in the article did you find interesting/unusual/surprising?
3 Imagine you can live another person's life for one day. Whose life would you choose?

A Day in a Life

What did you do yesterday? Tell us about your life.

1 ....

I am a Sami Norwegian, and I live 300 kilometers north of the Arctic Circle. In the winter, I go to school with my friends in Tromsø. But in the summer, the Sami people work with reindeer, so my life is very different. Yesterday I helped my family with calf marking. We were checking our herd of reindeer and making special marks in their ears to show that they belong to our family. In the past, my family followed our herd of reindeer on wooden skis, but now we travel by snowmobile! While I was helping with the calf marking, I sent two texts to my friends in Tromsø.

Flora Turi, 15, Norway

2 ....

Yesterday was the same as every other day. I got up at 6 a.m., ate a very quick breakfast and then took the bus to school. When I got to school at seven thirty, my classmates were sweeping the classroom. I helped them, and we all sang our national anthem. Between 8 a.m. and noon, I was studying, studying, studying, and after lunch, I had more classes until 4:30 p.m. Did I go home at 4:30 p.m.? No, I didn't! I stayed at school for an extra study hall. And then I went to another school for more classes. When I finally got home, it was 10 p.m. I had some dinner, and I did my homework. For Taiwanese teenagers, life is all about studying!

Tao Chen, 16, Taiwan

3 ....

I live with my family in a beautiful part of Canada. We live "off the grid"—that means that we have no electricity in our house. We don't have the Internet and we don't have phones, but we do have a radio in case of emergencies. I don't go to school—I'm homeschooled—but I learn a lot from my off-the-grid life. Yesterday I worked with my dad. We were looking at his designs for a new windmill. In the afternoon, I did some homework. I was researching some facts for a history project with other homeschooled kids. Of course, we didn't use the Internet for our research; we used an encyclopedia and other books from the local library.

Tom Renwood, 15, Canada

Grammar • Past simple vs Past continuous

Past simple	Past continuous
I got up at 6 a.m. We didn't use the Internet for my project.	We were checking our herd of reindeer. Between 8 a.m. and noon, I was studying.

Past simple and Past continuous

When I got to school, my classmates were sweeping the classroom.
While I was helping, I sent some texts to my friends in Tromsø.

Grammar reference Workbook page 86

Watch Out!
Some verbs, such as *know, understand, like, love, want, have* and *hear*, are stative verbs. They don't usually take the continuous form.
(For a full list, see page 43.)

1 Study the grammar table. Choose the correct options to complete the rules.

1 We use the *Past simple / Past continuous* for completed actions in the past.
2 We use the *Past simple / Past continuous* to describe a continuing situation in the past.
3 We usually use the *Past simple / Past continuous* after *when*, and the *Past simple / Past continuous* after *while*.

2 Complete the text with the correct form of the verbs.

Hi Ted,
I [1] *didn't have* (not have) a good day yesterday. First, I [2] .... (not hear) my alarm clock, and I [3] .... (sleep) until 8 o'clock. I was late for my first class. When I [4] .... (go) into the classroom, the teacher [5] .... (talk) about the homework. My classmates [6] .... (take) a lot of notes, but I [7] .... (not have) my notebook because I [8] .... (leave) my schoolbag at home. So the teacher [9] .... (shout) at me, and he [10] .... (give) me extra homework.
What about you? [11] .... (you/have) a good day yesterday?
Sam

3 Choose the correct options.

Last weekend my brother and I [1] *went / were going* for a bike ride. We [2] *took / were taking* a train to downtown Chicago, and then we [3] *rode / were riding* our bikes to Grant Park. While we [4] *rode / were riding* down the street, we [5] *saw / were seeing* a car crash. We [6] *stopped / were stopping* and [7] *called / were calling* an ambulance. When the ambulance [8] *arrived / was arriving*, the drivers [9] *sat / were sitting* on the pavement, and they [10] *argued / were arguing* about the accident.

4 Make sentences.

1 While we / watch / TV / we / hear / a strange sound
While we were watching TV, we heard a strange sound.
2 When you / call / I / do my homework
3 I / not hear / the doorbell / because / I / listen / to my MP3 player
4 I / see / a strange cat in the yard / while / I / wash / the car
5 She / drop / a plate / while / she / do / the dishes

5 What about you? In pairs, ask and answer the questions.

1 What did you do the day before yesterday?
2 What were you doing between 2 p.m. and 5 p.m. last Saturday?
3 Where did you go last weekend?
4 What did you see on your way to school today?
5 When did you last use your cell phone? Who were you talking to?

Vocabulary • Phrasal verbs 1

1 1.6 **Read the text and complete these phrasal verbs with the correct preposition. Then listen, check and repeat.**

1 count *on*
2 fill ....
3 find ....
4 get ....
5 give ....
6 go ....
7 hang ....
8 look ....
9 run ....
10 set ....

Word list page 43 **Workbook** page 104

I usually hang out with my friends in the summer and go out a lot. But last year I set up a dog-walking service with my sister. Customers could count on us to take their dogs for a walk anytime! Our favorite pet was a dog named Tyson. On his first walk, he ran away. We looked for him for several hours, but finally we gave up. We went to the police station and filled out a "missing pet" form. "What will the owner say when he finds out?" my sister asked. When we got back to the owner's house, we saw Tyson. He was waiting for us at the front door!

2 **Match the phrasal verbs to these definitions.**

1 to rely or depend on *count on*
2 to complete a form
3 to spend time in a place doing nothing
4 to escape
5 to discover or learn new information
6 to arrange or organize
7 to stop doing something
8 to return
9 to search
10 to leave home to go to a social event

3 1.7 **Match the pictures (a–e) to the conversations (1–5). Then complete them with the correct form of the phrasal verbs. Listen and check your answers.**

1 **A** Can I [1] *count on* you to watch your little sister this afternoon? I have a meeting in New York.
B OK, but please don't [2] .... late because I'm [3] .... to Tanya's birthday party in the evening.

2 **A** What did you do yesterday? Did you [4] .... with your friends in the park?
B No, I didn't. I went online and [5] .... a Facebook page for my band.

3 **A** I'm trying to [6] .... this form online, but my computer isn't working. I can't do it!
B Don't [7] .... ! Print out the form and mail it.

4 **A** My cat [8] .... yesterday. He got on the bus and traveled around town.
B How did you [9] .... where he was?
A The bus driver saw the tag on his collar and called me.

5 **A** Are you [10] .... something?
B Yes, I am. I can't find my favorite T-shirt!

4 **Work in pairs. Choose at least four phrasal verbs from Exercise 1 and write a short conversation.**

Brain Trainer Unit 1
Activity 3
Go to page 112

Chatroom Expressing extremes

Speaking and Listening

1 **Look at the photo. Can you remember how the girls know each other?**

2 **Listen and read the conversation. Check your answer.** 1.8

3 **Listen and read again. Answer the questions.** 1.8

1 Why is Yasmin in Concord?
She lives there now.
2 What does she think of it?
3 What does Archie think of the town?
4 What does Yasmin's mom do?
5 Does Yasmin's house have an amazing yard?

4 **Act out the conversation in groups of four.**

Holly Hi, Fraser! Hi, Archie! This is my cousin, Yasmin.
Archie Hey, Yasmin. We met last summer, remember?
Yasmin Yes, of course. And now I live here! I love Concord. It's such a cool town!
Archie Cool! I don't think so. It's really boring. It's so small, and there's nothing to do in the evening.
Yasmin Well, I used to live in a really busy city, and I hated it. It was so noisy.
Fraser Why did your family move here?
Yasmin My mom wanted to get out of the city. She used to have such a stressful job, but she gave it up and set up her own business as a landscape designer.
Fraser So do you live in a house with an amazing yard now?
Yasmin Yeah, right! It's a junkyard. But Mom has a lot of plans.

Say it in your language ...
I don't think so!
Yeah, right!

5 **Find and complete these sentences with *so* or *such*. Which word comes before an adjective without a noun?**

1 It's *such* a cool town!
2 It's .... small, and there's nothing to do in the evening.
3 It was .... noisy.
4 She used to have .... a stressful job.

6 **Read the phrases for expressing extremes.**

Expressing extremes	
so	It was **so** noisy. The skyscrapers are **so** tall. I'm **so** hungry.
such	It's **such** a cool town! He's **such** a nice man. It's **such** a hot day today.
really	It's **really** boring. I used to live in a **really** busy city.

7 1.9 **Listen to the conversations. Act out the conversations in pairs.**

Holly I love this [1] movie. It's so [2] funny!
Yasmin I agree. And [3] Amy Poehler is such a [4] great actor.

Archie You have such a [5] big house, Fraser.
Fraser It is [6] big, but [7] it's so chilly in the winter.

8 **Work in pairs. Replace the words in purple in Exercise 7. Use these words and/or your own ideas. Act out the conversations.**

1 band / book
2 talented / exciting
3 Adam Levine / the author
4 good singer / wonderful writer
5 nice room / small phone
6 beautiful / small
7 hot in summer / difficult to use

Grammar • Used to

Affirmative		
I/He/She/We/You/They	used to	live in a big city.
Negative		
I/He/She/We/You/They	didn't use to	have a car.
Questions and short answers		
Did I/he/she/we/you/they use to read comics when I/he/she/we/you/they was/were younger?	Yes, I/he/she/we/you/they did.	
	No, I/he/she/we/you/they didn't.	
***Wh* questions**		
Who used to teach English at this school?		

Grammar reference Workbook page 86

1 **Study the grammar table. Complete the rules with *used to* or *use to* and choose the correct options.**

1 We use .... to talk about *habits / completed actions* in the past.
2 We form the positive with .... + infinitive.
3 We form the negative with *didn't* and .... + infinitive.
4 We form questions with *Did* + subject + ... + infinitive.

2 **Complete the sentences with the correct form of *used to* and the verbs in parentheses.**

1 My sister *used to love* (love) chocolate, but now she hates it.
2 I .... (not walk) to school, but now I walk there every day.
3 Where did you .... (go) on vacation?
4 **A** .... (you be) on the basketball team?
B Yes, I did. But I .... (not enjoy) it.
5 We .... (not spend) much time in the park.
6 What .... (you do) after school when you lived in Detroit?

3 **Complete these sentences with your own ideas.**

1 When I was five, I didn't use to …
2 I always used to like … , but now …
3 My family used to … , but now …

Reading

1 Read the article quickly. Which sentence is the best summary of the article?

1 Ezekiel Barzey started The Golden Company because he was scared of bees.
2 Ezekiel Barzey's experience of beekeeping changed his life.
3 Ezekiel Barzey used to work for a bank, but now he makes honey.

Ezekiel, the Bee Guardian

"I used to be a completely different person," says Ezekiel Barzey, age 19. "I used to hang out with my friends, and we got into trouble with the police. I felt excluded, and I only saw the negative things in my community." But when Ezekiel was 17 years old, he got involved in a project run by Zoe Palmer, and his life began to change.

Zoe used to be a moviemaker for a TV nature channel, and she spent some time in Albania, filming bees and beekeepers. She was impressed by the relaxed and calm atmosphere around the beekeepers. When she got back to Britain, she set up The Golden Company. It teaches young people in London about beekeeping and gives them the opportunity to connect with nature and to find out how to develop, market and sell honey products.

Ezekiel is now a "Bee Guardian," and he takes care of a hive on the roof garden of the Nomura Investment Bank, in the heart of the City of London. The bank buys all the honey and uses it at meetings and business breakfasts. There are several other hives in London, and they all have special Bee Guardians from The Golden Company. Ezekiel also helps to run a stand at a local market in the city. He and other Bee Guardians make beauty products from honey and sell them at the stand.

Ezekiel was scared of the bees when he started his training, but he learned to calm down and not to panic. Now the bees can count on him to take care of them. "I'm more in touch with nature now," he explains. "I understand how bees operate!" He is also much more confident about himself and his role in society. "Now I have a chance in life to become successful," he says. "I'm glad the company was there for me when I needed it."

Key Words

excluded
get involved
beekeeping/beekeeper
honey
hive
stand

2 Read the article again. Answer the questions.
1.10

1 Why did Ezekiel's life change when he was 17 years old?
Because he got involved in a project run by Zoe Palmer.
2 What impressed Zoe Palmer in Albania?
3 What is The Golden Company?
4 Where is the hive that Ezekiel takes care of?
5 How does the bank use the honey?
6 What do Ezekiel and the other Bee Guardians make from the honey?
7 How did Ezekiel's feelings about bees change?
8 How did Ezekiel's feelings about himself change?

Listening

1 Listen to the radio show and choose the correct summary.
1.11

1 Laura taught the trumpet, and changed someone's life.
2 Laura heard the trumpet, and it changed her life.
3 Laura found a trumpet on the street, and it changed her life.

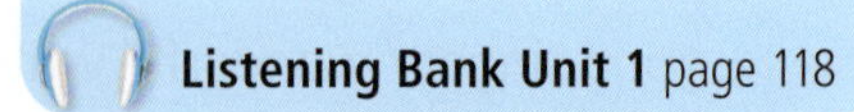
Listening Bank Unit 1 page 118

2 Think about a famous person, for example, a sports star, a musician or an actor, and imagine how that person chose his/her career.

1 What important moment do you imagine changed his/her life? Why was it important?
2 Was there an important moment in your life that changed you? How? What happened?

Writing • Telling a story

1 Read the Writing File.

Writing File Using different tenses

We often use a mix of tenses when we tell a story in the past.

- **We use the Past simple to describe a series of events.**
  I jumped out of bed, got dressed and went down to the kitchen.
- **We use the Past continuous for descriptions and continuous actions.**
  It was raining and a dog was barking.
- **We use the Present simple in dialogues and to describe states and things that don't change.**
  "I don't feel well today," she said.
  My family lives in a small house near the ocean.

2 Make sentences. Choose the correct tense from Exercise 1.

1 Last weekend / I / visit / my aunt / and then / I / go / to the movies
Last weekend I visited my aunt, and then I went to the movies.
2 I / usually / get up / at 7 o'clock
3 Yesterday afternoon / my sister / read / a magazine / when / the doorbell / ring
4 "you / like / chocolate?" asked my teacher

3 Read the story on the right. Find these tenses.

- Present simple
- Past simple
- Present continuous
- Past continuous

4 Read the story again. Answer the questions.

1 What did Gina do after she got up?
She had breakfast and helped her dad in the yard.
2 Was the weather good or bad?
3 Why was Gina not happy?
4 What is Gina always doing?
5 What prize did Gina win?
6 Where does Gina's family usually go on vacation?

An Amazing Day by Gina Bett

Yesterday was an amazing day. It began as usual—a typical boring Saturday. I got up, had breakfast and helped my dad in the yard. The sun was shining, and the birds were singing in the sky, but I was in a bad mood because I had a lot of homework, and I wanted to go out with my friends. Then my mom came outside. She was holding a letter.

"It's for you!" she said.

I read the letter quickly and shouted, "I don't believe it!"

"What is it?" asked my mom.

"I entered a contest last week," I replied, "Do you remember?"

Well, of course she didn't remember. I'm always entering contests, and I never win anything.

But this time it was different.

"I won first prize," I said. "A family vacation in Florida!"

We all shouted and laughed. Then we ran inside and started to plan our vacation. We usually go camping in the rain—but not this year!

5 You are going to write a short story with the title *An Unusual Day*. Plan your story. Think about these things.

- Who are the main characters in the story?
- What happens to them?
- How do they feel?
- What happens at the end of the story?

6 Now write your story. Use your ideas from Exercise 5.

Remember!

- Use a mix of tenses.
- Use the vocabulary in this unit.
- Check your grammar, spelling and punctuation.

Refresh Your Memory!

Grammar • Review

1 Match the sentence beginnings (1–5) to the endings (a–e).

1 The sun was shining brightly, *b*
2 When I got to the bus stop,
3 I sat down
4 I was waiting for the bus
5 While I was running toward the child,

a I dropped my bag.
b and the birds were singing.
c and waited for the next bus.
d the bus was already disappearing down the street.
e when I saw a child in the middle of the street.

2 Complete the text with the correct form of the verbs, Past simple or Past continuous.

I [1] *was eating* (eat) my lunch when the phone [2] .... (ring). I [3] .... (stand) up quickly and [4] .... (run) toward the phone. While I [5] .... (run), I [6] .... (trip) over the dog and [7] .... (hurt) my leg. I [8] .... (try) to stand up again when I [9] .... (hear) the doorbell. I [10] .... (walk) slowly to the door and [11] .... (open) it. It was my friend, Kate. "Are you OK?" she asked. "You [12] .... (not/answer) the phone."

3 Make sentences with *used to* and *didn't use to* and the information in the chart.

When John was five …

play soccer	✗
be scared of the dark	✓
believe in ghosts	✓
have a lot of homework	✗
ride a bike to school	✗
like chocolate	✓
climb trees in the park	✓

When John was five, he didn't use to play soccer.

Vocabulary • Review

4 Match the words in box *a* to the words in box *b* to make compound nouns.

a baby*sitter* business class fire home light sky snow space speed white wind

b board boat fighter house mate mill mobile person scraper ship ~~sitter~~ work

5 Complete the sentences with the correct form of these phrasal verbs.

count on fill out get back give up go out hang out look for ~~set up~~

1 My mother *set up* her own travel company when she was 20 years old.
2 I know that the homework is difficult, but don't .... !
3 Please .... this form to apply for the job.
4 I .... my jacket in my bedroom, but I couldn't find it.
5 Last night we .... to a few clubs downtown.
6 When you need help, you can always .... me.
7 I usually .... with my friends on the weekend.
8 I usually .... from school at 4 o'clock.

Speaking • Review

6 Complete the conversation with the correct words. Then listen and check. 1.12

A I don't like this town. It's [1] *so* / *such* boring!
B I don't agree. I think it's [2] *such* / *really* great. It has [3] *such* / *really* a fantastic park, and the gym is [4] *so* / *such* cheap.
A Well, that's true. But we live [5] *so* / *such* a long way from the center of town. And the buses are [6] *so* / *such* expensive.
B True, but you have a [7] *so* / *really* big house with a nice yard. You're [8] *so* / *such* lucky!

Dictation

7 Listen and write in your notebook. 1.13

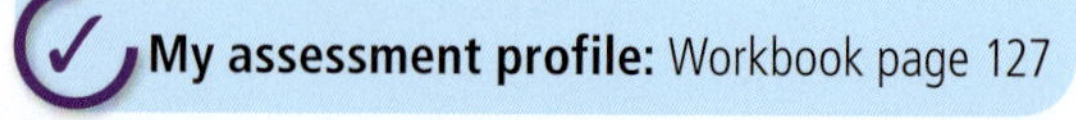

My assessment profile: Workbook page 127

Biology File

Where Are All the Bees?

1 .c.. All around the world, reports warn that bees are flying away from their hives and not returning. Farmers, scientists and environmental groups are worried, and they are trying to find out why it's happening.

2 .... Are they so important to our environment? The short answer is yes, it does matter, and yes, they are important. Bees fly around from flower to flower, looking for nectar and pollen. They use these to produce honey, which is food for their colonies. But at the same time, the bees help to move pollen from one flower to another. This process is called "pollination." Pollination means that the flowers can create seeds and new flowers. Without bees, many flowers can't make seeds or fruit. In fact, bees are responsible for the pollination of one-third of all of the plants that we eat. A single hive with 50,000 honeybees can pollinate 500,000 plants in one day! Imagine a world with no apples, carrots, onions, raspberries, strawberries or, of course, honey. That's a world with no bees.

3 .... Scientists think that there are several possible reasons, including climate change, disease and pesticides (chemicals that kill insects).

4 .... Beekeeping was popular two or three hundred years ago, when many families kept their own hives for honey. Now beekeeping is becoming popular again in towns and cities, as well as in the country. In fact, towns are actually good places for hives because they have gardens and parks with a lot of different types of flowers. Elementary schools, businesses, universities and community centers are now setting up their own hives. They enjoy the delicious honey, and at the same time they know that they are helping to take care of some of the most important insects on the planet.

Reading

1 Read the article quickly. Match these sentences to the correct paragraphs.

a But it's not all bad news.
b But does it really matter if bees disappear?
c Bees are disappearing.
d So, why are the bees disappearing?

2 Read the article again. Answer the questions. 1.14

1 Why are farmers, scientists and environmental groups worried about bees?
2 Why do bees fly from one flower to another?
3 What is pollination?
4 How many plants can one bee pollinate in one day?
5 What possible causes are there for the bees' disappearance?
6 Why are towns good environments for beekeeping?

3 Listen to some more information on bees. Choose the correct numbers to complete the fact file. 1.15

6.5   6   4,000   one-twelfth ($^1/_{12}$)   ~~25,000~~   24

Bee Fact File — Did you know ...?

- There are around [1] 25,000 species of bees in the world.
- There are over [2] .... species of bees in the US.
- A bee produces [3] .... of a teaspoon of honey in its life.
- The average life of a worker bee is [4] .... weeks.
- Bees fly [5] .... kilometers on an average trip.
- They can fly [6] .... kilometers per hour.

My Biology File

4 You are going to produce a pamphlet about butterflies. Find out the following information about them.

- How they find food
- Why they are important for the environment
- If they face the same problems as bees
- How we can protect them
- How many species there are in the world/in your country

5 Work in pairs and make your pamphlet. Include pictures or photos if possible.

2 Aiming High

Grammar
Present perfect; Present perfect vs Past simple

Vocabulary
Collocations with *make*, *go* and *keep*; Jobs and suffixes

Speaking
Giving/Responding to news

Writing
A biography

Word list page 43
Workbook page 105

Vocabulary • Collocations with *make*, *go* and *keep*

1 1.16 **Copy the table. Put these phrases under the correct verbs. Then listen, check and repeat.**

~~a decision~~
a difference
a secret
calm
control
crazy
for a walk
in touch
it to the finals
together
someone's dream come true
well

make	keep	go
a decision	....	....

2 **Match the phrases from Exercise 1 to the definitions.**

1 not tell someone about something *keep a secret*
2 become very excited about something or be very impractical
3 combine well with something
4 succeed in a sport so that you will play in the most important game
5 have an important effect on something
6 communicate with someone
7 choose to do something
8 achieve an ambition or a hope
9 make a short journey on foot
10 manage
11 don't get angry or upset
12 happen in a good way

3 1.17 **Complete the cartoons with the correct form of a collocation from Exercise 1. Then listen and check your answers.**

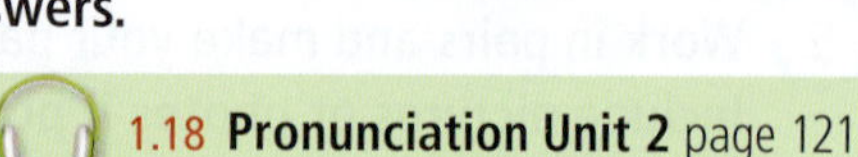
1.18 **Pronunciation Unit 2** page 121

1 Hannah goes *crazy* every time she hears One Direction.

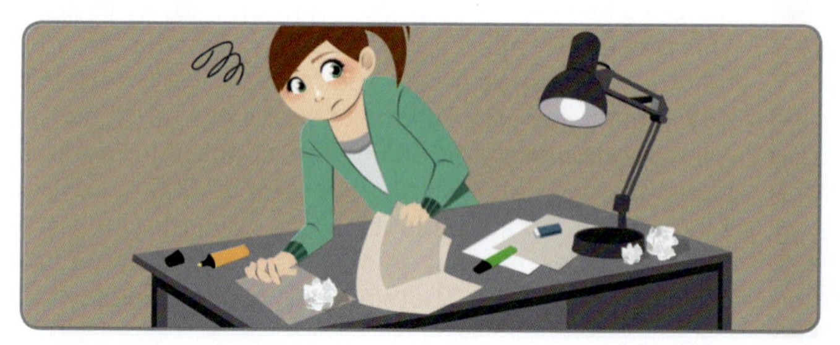

2 This morning is not going ....! I can't find my favorite One Direction CD.

3 It's a surprise present for your sister. Can you keep ....?

4 I can't believe it! You made ....!

Brain Trainer Unit 2
Activities 1 and 2
Go to pages 112–113

Reading

1 **Look at the large photo. In pairs, discuss. Why is this soccer field unusual? Where do you think it is?**

2 **Read the article quickly and put the events (a–e) in the correct order.**

a Panyee SC won the Youth Soccer Tournament.
b The boys built a soccer field.
c The boys were watching the World Cup on TV. *1*
d Panyee SC got to the semifinals of a local soccer tournament.
e The boys practiced their soccer skills on the wooden field.

3 **Read the article again. Answer the questions.**
1.19

1 What is the main industry of Koh Panyee? *fishing*
2 How many families live on Koh Panyee?
3 What inspired the boys to form a soccer team?
4 Why did the villagers laugh at the boys?
5 What materials did the boys use to make the soccer field?
6 How did the boys become so good at soccer?

4 **What about you? In pairs, ask and answer.**

- What sports facilities do you have in your town or city?
- Can you think of ways to improve them?
- Do you know of any other unusual places where people play sports?

Making Dreams Come True

In a small fishing village in southern Thailand, some boys enthusiastically play soccer. They run, shout, jump and kick like most other soccer players, but these boys are especially good at keeping control of the ball. Why? Because their soccer field is a raft in the middle of the ocean! They live on the island of Koh Panyee, where all the houses are on stilts. The island has a total population of three hundred families, but although the village is small, its success on the soccer field has been huge. Since 2004, the Panyee Soccer Club has won the Thai Youth Soccer Tournament seven times.

The story of Panyee SC begins back in 1986. Some of the young boys from the village were watching the World Cup Soccer Tournament on television. Suddenly, one of the boys said, "We watch soccer on TV, but we've never played it." The boys made a decision. "Our soccer team starts today. We want to become world champions!" they shouted. But the villagers laughed at them. "Are you crazy? Have you ever played soccer?" they asked. "You've already formed a team, but you haven't found a field yet! How can you practice?" The boys were determined to make their dream come true. They used old fishing boats and pieces of wood to make a floating soccer field. They practiced for hours every day, even when the field was wet, and developed amazing skills. That first year, they made it to the semifinals of the local soccer tournament. Panyee SC has now played for over twenty-five years and is one of the best youth soccer teams in the country.

Grammar • Present perfect

Present perfect + *ever, never, already, yet*
The village's success on the soccer field has been huge.
Have you ever played soccer?
We watch soccer on TV, but we have never played it.
You've already formed a soccer team, but you haven't found a field yet!

Grammar reference Workbook page 88

Watch Out!
Ever, never and *already* come between *have/has* and the main verb. *Yet* comes at the end of the sentence.
I've never been to a soccer game.
The team hasn't scored a goal yet.

1 **Study the grammar table and Watch Out! Complete the rules with these words.**

already ever never yet

1 We use .... with questions. It means "at any time."
2 .... means "at no time."
3 .... means "earlier than expected."
4 (not) .... means that something we expected to happen has not happened at that point.

2 **Make questions with *ever.* Answer the questions.**

1 you / play / beach volleyball?
Have you ever played beach volleyball?
Yes, I have./No, I haven't.
2 you / sleep / on a train?
3 your family / travel / to Africa?
4 you / swim / in the ocean?
5 you / meet / a famous actor?

3 **Choose the correct options.**

Joe Didn't you need to call your aunt, Tom?
Tom I've [1] *already / ever* talked to her. And guess what? She gave my brother and me tickets to watch the Chicago Cubs at Wrigley Field!
Joe Wow! I've [2] *never / ever* been to Wrigley Field. You're so lucky.
Tom I know! I haven't told my brother [3] *ever / yet.* He's [4] *yet / already* gone to bed because he doesn't feel well.
Joe Have you [5] *already / ever* been to a Cubs game before?
Tom Yes, I saw them play last year. It was amazing!

Present perfect with *since* and *for*
Since 2004, the Panyee Soccer Club has won the Thai Youth Soccer Tournament seven times.
Panyee SC has now played for over twenty-five years.

4 **Read the grammar table and choose the correct options.**

1 We use the Present perfect with *for / since* to talk about a period of time.
2 We use the Present perfect with *for / since* to talk about something that started at a point in time in the past.

5 **Copy the table and put these time words/phrases in the correct column.**

ever, last summer, several years, 2010, a few minutes, the last time I saw you, she was a child, ~~two weeks~~, ~~my birthday~~, two hours

for	since
two weeks	*my birthday*

6 **What about you? In pairs, ask and answer.**

1 What have you already done today?
2 What important things have you not done yet this week?
3 How many text messages have you sent since yesterday?
4 What have you never done, but want to do?

Vocabulary • Jobs and suffixes *-or, -er, -ist*

1 1.20 **Match these words to the items in the picture (1–12). Then listen, check and repeat.**

art	artist	novel	novelist
photograph	photographer	play	playwright
poem	poet	sculptor	sculpture *1*

Word list page 43
Workbook page 105

2 **Match the pairs of words from Exercise 1.**

art	*artist*
novel	....
photograph	....
play	....
poem	....
sculpture	....

3 **Use the suffixes *-or*, *-er* or *-ist* to make more jobs. In your notebook, draw wordwebs like this one to record your words.**

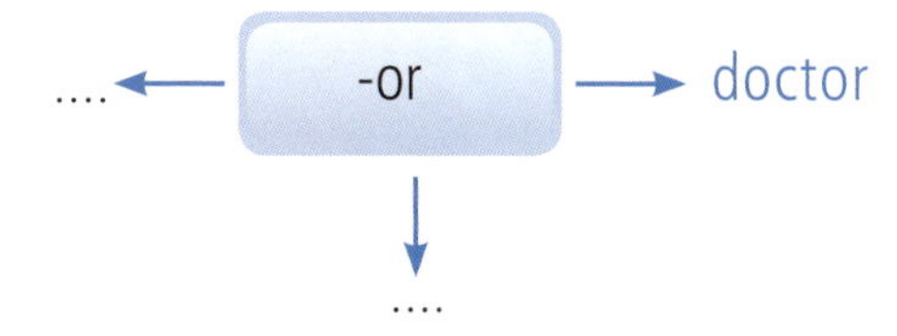

4 **Work in pairs. Choose a job from Exercise 1 or 3. Say three words related to the job, but don't use the word itself. Can your partner guess the job?**

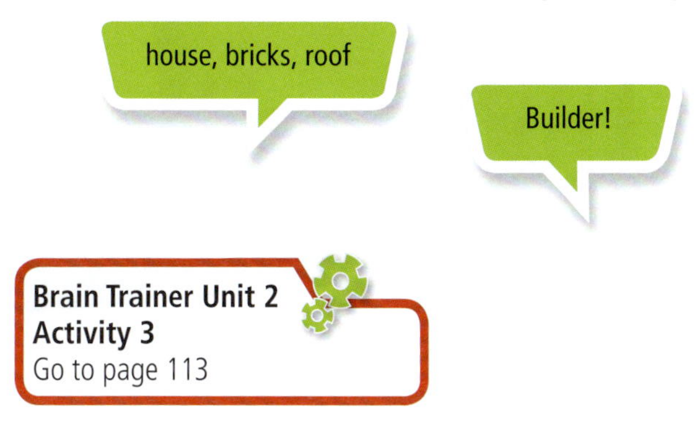

Brain Trainer Unit 2
Activity 3
Go to page 113

Chatroom Giving/Responding to news

Speaking and Listening

1 **Look at the photo. Who has been playing Frisbee?**

2 **Listen and read the conversation.**
1.21 **Check your answer.**

3 **Listen and read again. Answer the questions.**
1.21
1 Who is probably worse at playing Frisbee than Yasmin? *Archie*
2 Who is Mr. Turnbull?
3 What has Mr. Turnbull just won?
4 Does Holly think that Mr. Turnbull is a good singer?
5 Why is Fraser surprised about the chocolate bar advertisement?

4 **Act out the conversation in groups of four.**

Yasmin I dropped it again. I'm a lost cause!
Holly You've never played with Archie! He can't catch to save his life!
Fraser Shh! Look, he's over there. He's waving at us. You're late, Archie. What's up?
Archie You'll never believe this!
Holly What?
Archie I just heard some amazing news.
Yasmin Yeah? Come on, what happened?
Archie Well, I was reading the paper, and you won't believe it, but Mr. Turnbull, the soccer coach, has won a national songwriting contest.
Yasmin No way!
Holly Mr. Turnbull, a songwriter? You're kidding me! He looks like he can't even sing in tune.
Archie Seriously. I swear it's true. He wrote the music for a chocolate bar advertisement on TV last year.
Fraser Unbelievable! And he's always saying that chocolate is bad for us!

Say it in your language ...
I'm a lost cause!
He can't catch to save his life!

5 **Look back at the conversation. Find these expressions.**

1 Two ways to say: *Tell me about it.*
What's up?
2 Three ways to say: *I don't believe you!*
3 One way to say: *It's true.*

6 **Read the phrases for giving and responding to news.**

Giving news
I just heard some amazing news.
You won't believe it, but …
Asking about news
What's up?
What happened?
Responding to news
No way!
You're kidding me!
Unbelievable!
Confiming news
Seriously.
I swear it's true.

7 1.22 **Listen to the conversations. Act out the conversations in pairs.**

Yasmin I just heard some amazing news!
Fraser What happened?
Yasmin [1] My uncle just got a job as principal of our school.
Fraser No way!

Holly You won't believe it, but [2] I won first prize in a poetry contest.
Archie You're kidding me!
Holly Seriously.

Yasmin What's up, Fraser?
Fraser [3] I just found twenty bucks in my pocket.
Yasmin Unbelievable!

8 **Work in pairs and practice the conversations in Exercise 7. Replace the words in purple. Use these phrases and/or your own ideas.**

1 my brother / get into drama school
2 my dog / win / first prize in a pet show
3 my dad / buy a Porsche

Grammar • Present perfect vs Past simple

Present perfect
Mr. Turnbull has won a songwriting contest.
Past simple
He wrote the music for a chocolate bar advertisement on TV last year.

Grammar reference Workbook page 88

1 **Study the grammar table. Choose the correct options to complete the rules.**

1 We use the *Past simple / Present perfect* to talk about an action at an unspecified time in the past or in an unfinished time period that has a result in the present.
2 We use the *Past simple / Present perfect* to talk about an action at a specified time in the past.

2 **Complete the sentences. Use the Present perfect or Past simple form of the verbs.**

1 Yesterday I *got up* (get up) early and *went* (go) for a run before breakfast.
2 We …. (not see) Mark since last Christmas.
3 They …. (not watch) a DVD yesterday; they …. (listen) to some music.
4 …. (you/see) the new Batman movie? It's awesome!

3 **Complete the news report with the correct form of these verbs.**

break	join	never win
take part in	teach	~~win~~

Schoolteacher Is Swimming Star!

Math teacher Sarah Lee [1] *has won* an international swim meet. Ms. Lee [2] …. Fairbridge School two months ago, but she also works at Goldfins Swimming Club, where she [3] …. swimming for several years. On January 22 she [4] …. the 800 meters freestyle swimming record. "I [5] …. in hundreds of swim meets since I was a child," said Ms. Lee, "but I [6] …. a medal before!"

4 **Work in pairs. Imagine you have achieved something amazing! Interview each other. Use the Present perfect and Past simple.**

It's Never Too Soon ... to Aim for Success

Nancy Yi Fan was just 11 years old in 2004 when she started to write *Swordbird*—a fantasy novel about birds. She spent two years writing it, and then emailed the book to several large publishing companies in the US. Just one month later, in 2006, Nancy had a publishing deal and became one of the youngest published novelists in the US. But what makes Nancy's achievement even more impressive is the fact that English isn't her first language. Nancy was born to Chinese parents in China, and the family moved to the US when she was seven years old. In 2008 *Swordbird* reached the top of the *New York Times* bestseller list. Nancy has now written a prequel to *Swordbird*, called *Sword Quest,* and she's also translated *Swordbird* into Chinese!

It's Never Too Late ... to Learn Something New

In 1989 a gallery in Sydney, Australia, presented an exhibition of Aboriginal art. The exhibition was a huge success, and many art dealers and gallery owners became particularly interested in one of the artists there—Emily Kngwarreye. This artist's painting, *Emu Woman*, was the image on the front cover of the exhibition catalogue. The art world of Australia wanted to know more about this extraordinary artist. "Who is she?" they wondered. "What else has she already painted?" Amazingly, Kngwarreye was a 79-year-old Aboriginal woman, and *Emu Woman* was her first ever painting on canvas. In the following eight years, Kngwarreye produced nearly 3,000 paintings (approximately one painting per day). She died in 1999, and is now one of Australia's most famous abstract artists. Her paintings have become famous around the world. Not a bad achievement for an artist who only began painting at the age of 78!

Key Words

publishing deal, impressive, bestseller, art dealer, gallery owner, canvas

Reading

1 Read the article quickly. Choose the correct option.

1. Nancy/Emily became famous at the age of 79.
2. Nancy/Emily has written two books.
3. Nancy/Emily is alive today.
4. Nancy/Emily produced thousands of paintings.

2 (1.23) Read the article again. Find the important events for these dates.

1. 1989
   There was an exhibition of Aboriginal art in Sydney, Australia.
2. 1999
3. 2004
4. 2006
5. 2008

Listening

1 (1.24) Listen to the news show and match the people (1–4) to the descriptions (a–d).

1 Raj Patel	a US talk show host
2 Nisha Patel	b musician
3 Jennifer Marquez	c student
4 Larry Nixon	d actor

Listening Bank Unit 2 page 118

2 In pairs, ask and answer.

1. Do you like listening to rap music?
2. Have you ever tried to write a rap song?
3. What kind of music videos do you like to watch?
4. Have you ever uploaded a video online? What did the video present?

Writing • A biography

1 Read the Writing File.

Writing File Time expressions

When you write about a person's life, you can use different expressions of time.

- ***... years/months ago***
  Twenty-five years ago, Henry lived in a small house in the country.
- ***during* + period of time**
  During his childhood, he became interested in poetry.
- ***when* + pronoun + *was***
  When Henry was 12 years old, he won a national poetry contest.
- ***in* + year/month**
  In 2006 he decided to move to Nigeria.
- ***the following year/month***
  The following year, he met Jodie Taylor.
- **period of time + *later***
  Two years later, they got married.
- ***after* + period of time**
  After several months, they set up an online business.

2 Complete the sentences with the correct time word from the box.

after during following ~~in~~ when

1 My aunt was born *in* 1967.
2 .... she was 17 years old, she left school and traveled to India.
3 .... her stay in India, she worked for the "Save the Children" charity.
4 .... three years in India, she decided to return to the US and set up her own charity.
5 The .... year, she organized a charity fashion show in New York.

3 Read the biography and find the time expressions.

Katy Perry was born as Katheryn Elizabeth Hudson in *1984* in Santa Barbara, California. Her parents worked as Christian pastors, and her family wasn't very musical. But Katy often sang in her parents' church during her childhood.

When Katy was 17 years old, she moved to Los Angeles to start a career in music. It was a difficult time for her. She lived on her own, and she worked hard to get a deal in a record company, but she wasn't successful.

Five years later, in 2007, the recording company Capitol offered her a contract. In 2008 Katy's first album, *One of the Boys*, came out, and it was a huge success.

Katy released her second album, *Teenage Dream*, in 2010. Three years later, her third album, *Prism*, came out. Katy Perry is a true star now, and she has won many awards for her amazing, fun music.

4 Read the biography again and complete the timeline.

1984	Katy Perry was born.
2001	She moved to Los Angeles.
	The recording company Capitol offered her a contract.
2008	
2010	
	She released her third album, *Prism*.

5 Make a timeline like the one in Exercise 4. Make it about a family member or a famous person.

6 Write a biography. Use your timeline in Exercise 5 and the sample biography in Exercise 3 to help you.

Remember!
- Use expressions of time.
- Use the vocabulary in this unit.
- Check your grammar, spelling and punctuation.

Refresh Your Memory!

Grammar • Review

1 Complete the sentences with *already, ever, never* or *yet*.

1 **A** Have you *ever* met a famous actor?
B No, I haven't.
2 **A** Why aren't you laughing?
B Because I've .... heard that joke.
3 **A** Have you read that magazine .... ?
B Yes, I have.
4 **A** Have you started your history homework ....?
B Yes, I've .... finished it. I did it yesterday.
5 **A** Have you guys been to the new pool .... ?
B No. My brother has .... been swimming. He's scared of the water.

2 Choose the correct options.

1 My family has lived in this town *for* / *since* 2008.
2 I haven't seen him *for* / *since* last Christmas.
3 James stayed with us *for* / *since* two weeks over the summer.
4 She's been crazy about music *for* / *since* she was three years old.
5 The girls played tennis yesterday *for* / *since* two hours.

3 Complete the email with the correct form of the verbs.

Unread Message

Hi Sarah,
How are you?
[1] *Have you met* (you/meet) my friend Sophie? She lives next to my school. She [2] .... (just/hear) some amazing news—she [3] .... (get) into the Lincoln Arts School! She [4] .... (go) to the school for an audition last month. She [5] .... (sing) a song and [6] .... (play) the violin. She was so nervous! She [7] .... (not hear) anything from them for two weeks, but then yesterday she [8] .... (get) a letter from the school with an offer of admission. I'm so jealous!
Kate xx

REPLY

Vocabulary • Review

4 Complete the sentences with these words.

a decision	a difference	calm	control
~~crazy~~	for a walk	in touch	it to the finals
together	well		

1 Why are you riding your bike in the house? Have you gone *crazy*?
2 Is my outfit OK? Do you think brown and black go .... ?
3 What's the plan for this afternoon? We need to make .... soon.
4 We were so excited when our team made .... of the talent contest.
5 It's a beautiful day. Let's go .... in the park.
6 Please keep .... of your dog. He's in my yard!
7 Everyone looks bored. The party isn't going .... .
8 Ted lives in Italy, but he keeps .... by email.
9 A little kindness makes .... to other people.
10 Try to keep .... and don't panic!

5 Make jobs from these words.

art *artist*	novel	photograph
play	poem	sculpture

Speaking • Review

6 Complete the conversation with these words. Then listen and check. 1.25

~~I just heard~~	it's true	No way!
Seriously	What happened?	

A [1] *I just heard* some amazing news.
B Really? [2] ....
A My sister has won a car!
B [3] ....
A [4] .... . I swear [5].... .
B That's incredible!

Dictation

7 Listen and write in your notebook. 1.26

My assessment profile: Workbook page 128

Real World Profiles

Bruce Baillie Hamilton's Profile

Age
14 years old

Home country
Scotland

My favorite things…
languages, traveling, talking to people

The Polyglot

Bruce Baillie Hamilton, from Callander, Scotland, is only fourteen years old, but he's already a talented polyglot. Who or what is a polyglot? It's not an illness, or a strange animal; it's a term for someone who can speak several languages fluently. Bruce has recently won a contest to find "The Most Multilingual Child in the UK."

His first foreign languages were French and German, which he started learning at school when he was seven years old. At the age of nine, he decided to learn a language with a different alphabet and began to study Russian. It wasn't easy—"Russian grammar is really difficult," says Bruce—but he didn't stop. The next language was Chinese. "Chinese is interesting, even though it has no alphabet," says Bruce. "I found it hard at the beginning, but it gets easier. Now I think Chinese is the easiest of the languages to speak. When you are in China, and you can speak Chinese, the people are much friendlier."

He can also speak Spanish, Arabic and, of course, English, and he is planning to learn Lebanese Arabic soon.

Bruce is clearly a very talented and intelligent teenager, but he has also worked hard in order to learn these languages. Since the age of twelve, Bruce has spent about twenty hours a week of his free time on his language studies during the school year, and many more hours over summer breaks.

Bruce isn't the only talented linguist in his family. His brother, Angus, and his sister, Lucy, are both studying several foreign languages. It's a big surprise to his parents. "My husband and I are both awful at languages!" says his mother, Paula. "I am absolutely thrilled for Bruce. He's worked so hard, and he enjoys using the languages and communicating with them."

Reading

1 Read Bruce's profile and look at the title of the article. What is a polyglot? Guess. Then read the article quickly to check.

a a person who has traveled a lot
b a computer program to teach languages
c a person who can speak many languages
d a talkative person

2 Read the article again. Answer the questions. 1.27

1 How old was Bruce when he began to study French?
2 Why did he want to learn Russian?
3 What is unusual about the Chinese language?
4 What does Bruce say about the people in China?
5 Which language will Bruce learn next?
6 How much time does Bruce spend studying languages?
7 Why is Paula surprised that her children are good at languages?

Class discussion

1 Who can speak the most languages in your class?
2 What are the most commonly spoken languages in your country?
3 Which languages do you think are the most useful to learn? Why?

3 Be Happy!

Grammar
Gerunds and infinitives; Present perfect continuous

Vocabulary
Showing feelings; Adjective suffixes

Speaking
Invitations

Writing
A "for and against" essay

Word list page 43
Workbook page 106

Vocabulary • Showing feelings

1 **Match the pictures (1–6) to six words in the box.**

blush
cry
frown *1*
gasp
laugh
scream
shiver
shout
sigh *7*
smile
sweat
yawn

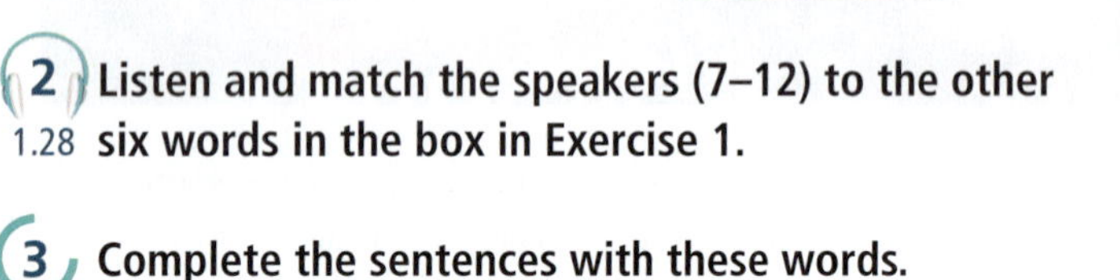

2 **Listen and match the speakers (7–12) to the other six words in the box in Exercise 1.**
1.28

3 **Complete the sentences with these words.**

gasp ~~shout~~ sigh sweat

1 We *shout* when we're angry.
2 We .... when we're very surprised.
3 We .... when we're hot.
4 We .... when we're fed up.

blush frown scream smile

5 We .... when we're frightened.
6 We .... when we're embarrassed.
7 We .... when we're in a bad mood.
8 We .... when we're happy.

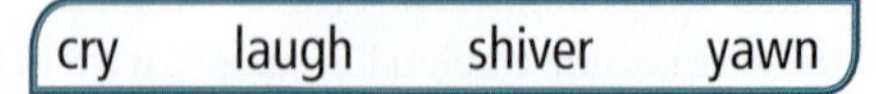
cry laugh shiver yawn

9 We .... when we're cold.
10 We .... when we're tired.
11 We .... when we're upset.
12 We .... when we're amused.

4 **When do you and your family do the things in Exercise 1?**
I often shiver when I get out of the swimming pool.
My mom sighs when she sees my messy room.

1.29 **Pronunciation Unit 3** page 121

Brain Trainer Unit 3
Activities 1 and 2
Go to page 113

Reading

1 Read the text quickly. Is it …

1 an advertisement? 2 an article? 3 a review?

2 Read the text again and answer the questions.

1.30

1. Which language can you use all around the world?
   You can use your smile all around the world.
2. Look at the pictures. Which picture do you think shows someone who
   - is not really happy?
   - is proud of something?
   - is amused?
3. What can people in a bad mood do to feel better? Find five ideas in the text.
4. What are endorphins?
5. According to the text, why do people often feel happier if you smile at them?

3 What about you? In pairs, ask and answer.

1. In what situations do people in your country smile at people they don't know?
2. How do you feel if someone gives you a fake smile?
3. How do you cheer yourself up when you're in a bad mood?
4. Think about something sad. Then think about the same thing and smile. Are your feelings the same or different?

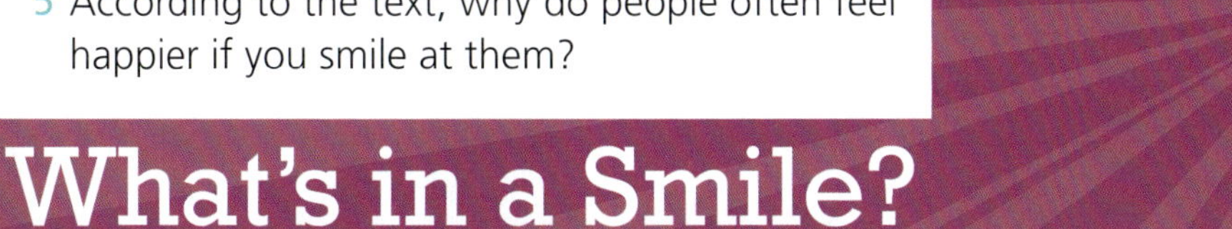

What's in a Smile?

You can't hope to learn all the world's languages, but there's one language that you can communicate with everywhere: your smile.

Smiling can show people that you're friendly and cheerful. According to scientists, however, we have more than fifty different types of smile for different situations. When something is funny, we usually smile with an open mouth. If we are proud of something, we keep our lips together. If our eyes become smaller when we smile, we are genuinely happy, but if the skin around our eyes doesn't move, our smile is fake. That's bad news in countries where people dislike a fake smile as much as a frown, like France and Russia.

But what if you are in a bad mood? It's hard to be cheerful all the time. Some people try to cheer themselves up by watching funny movies. Others prefer dancing to their favorite songs or eating chocolate. Others do sports every day to put themselves in a good mood. But there's another, very easy way to feel happier: smile. When you smile (even if it's a fake smile), your body starts producing chemicals called endorphins. Endorphins send a message to your brain that you are happy. And there's more. When you smile at people, they often smile back at you. This reaction produces endorphins in their body, and they feel happier, too. A part of their brain remembers you as a person who makes them happy. You're halfway to having a new friend. And that's definitely something you can smile about.

Grammar • Gerunds and infinitives

Gerunds
1 They cheer themselves up by watching funny movies.
2 Smiling can show people that you're friendly.
3 They prefer dancing to their favorite songs.
Infinitives
4 You can't hope to learn all the world's languages.
5 They do sports every day to put themselves in a good mood.
6 It's hard to be cheerful all the time.

Grammar reference Workbook page 90

1 Study the grammar table. Match the examples (1–6) to the uses (a–f).

We use **gerunds:**
a after certain verbs, e.g., *like, love, enjoy, hate, prefer, stop.*
b after prepositions.
c as the subject or object of a sentence.

We use **infinitives:**
d after certain verbs, e.g., *want, decide, hope, try, pretend, learn, remember, plan.*
e after certain adjectives, e.g., *easy, difficult, important, happy, sad, lucky.*
f when we are explaining the purpose of an action.

2 Choose the correct options.

Here are some of your ideas for [1] *being* / to be happy:
- [2] Spending / To spend time with my friends always makes me happy.
- Try [3] not wanting / not to want expensive gadgets. They can't bring you real happiness.
- I often go running [4] escaping / to escape my problems. I always feel better after a run.
- Remember [5] not being / not to be selfish. It's easier [6] becoming / to become happy by [7] helping / to help other people.
- I enjoy [8] watching / to watch comedies on TV. It's impossible [9] frowning / to frown when you're laughing!

3 Complete the sentences with the correct form of the verbs.

1 It's important *to have* (have) good friends.
2 Are you hoping .... (go) on vacation soon?
3 I hate .... (not be) at the same school as my sister.
4 Please stop .... (shout). You're giving me a headache!
5 It's hard .... (not feel) a little jealous of Lucy. She's so popular!
6 They want .... (relax) this weekend.
7 She's going to London .... (visit) her grandparents.
8 .... (play) table tennis is a lot of fun.

4 Complete the text with the correct form of these verbs.

do	feel	go	leave
meet	start	talk	~~work~~

Two years ago, my parents were tired of [1] *working* for big companies in New York. They decided [2] .... their jobs. We moved to a new home in the mountains [3] .... a new life. At first I didn't enjoy [4] .... to my new school. No one in my class wanted [5] .... to me. Then I joined the school's mountain sports club. I learned [6] .... sports like rock climbing and skiing, and it was easier [7] .... friendly people in the club. Soon I stopped [8] .... unhappy, and now I love my new home.

5 What about you? In pairs, ask and answer.

1 Which activities do you enjoy/not like doing?
2 What things are easy/difficult to do?
3 What are your plans and hopes for next year?

Bhutan

Bhutan is a small but beautiful country in the Himalayas. Its people are not wealthy—they live on less than five dollars a day. But they feel lucky. They have a king who tries to make them happy, not rich, and he is very successful. The Bhutanese are famous for being the happiest people in all of Asia.

They believe that people can't be happy if they aren't healthy, so Bhutan has good hospitals. It doesn't want factories that pollute the environment with poisonous chemicals. Before 1999, the king thought that TV was a dangerous influence and didn't allow it. Today people can watch TV, but there is more crime now in this peaceful country.

Vocabulary • Adjective suffixes

1 1.31 **Read the article and find the adjective forms of these nouns. Copy and complete the table. Then listen, check and repeat.**

~~beauty~~ danger fame health luck
peace poison success wealth

	Noun	Adjective
-ful	*beauty*	*beautiful*
-y	....	....
-ous	....	....

Word list page 43
Workbook page 106

2 Complete the sentences with words from Exercise 1.

1 There is no crime in this town. It's a very *peaceful* place.
2 Mom wished me good .... before the exam.
3 There are a lot of road accidents. Driving a car can be really .... .
4 He is so .... that he has a yacht!
5 She has a .... face, but she isn't tall enough to be a model.
6 Everyone knows Tom Cruise. He's a .... actor.
7 Don't eat those mushrooms. They're .... !
8 He has won a lot of races, but his .... in sports hasn't made him rich or famous.
9 She's very ....—she plays tennis every day and eats a lot of fruit.

3 In pairs, take turns saying a noun from Exercise 1. Your partner makes a sentence with the adjective form of the noun.

luck

My uncle is very lucky. He always wins money in the lottery.

Brain Trainer Unit 3
Activity 3
Go to page 114

Chatroom Invitations

Speaking and Listening

1 **Look at the photo. How is Fraser feeling? Why?**

2 **Listen and read the conversation.**
1.32 **Check your answer.**

3 **Listen and read again. Answer the questions.**
1.32
1 Why can't Archie and Holly go to the youth club?
Because they're going to Yasmin's party.
2 Why isn't Fraser going to the party?
3 Why does Yasmin call Fraser?
4 Why did Yasmin think she had invited Fraser to her party?
5 What does Fraser decide to do tonight?

4 **Act out the conversation in groups of four.**

Fraser Do you want to go to the youth club tonight?
Archie That sounds like fun, but I'm sorry, I can't. I'm going to Yasmin's party.
Fraser What about you, Holly? Do you feel like going?
Holly Sorry. I have to say no, too. Yasmin's been planning her party for months. It's going to be a great night.
Fraser It's not fair! I didn't even get an invitation … Oh, that's my phone. Hello?
Yasmin Fraser, hi, it's Yasmin. I've been calling you all day, but you never answer. Are you coming to my party? You haven't replied yet.
Fraser Well, you haven't invited me yet.
Yasmin Really? I thought I sent you a text last week.
Fraser I didn't get one.
Yasmin Oh, I'm such a lost cause! Sorry. Well, would you like to come? It's tonight at 7:30.
Fraser Sure! Thanks. I'll see you there.

Say it in your language …
It's not fair!
I'm such a lost cause!

5 **Look back at the conversation. Who says what?**

1 Do you want to go to the youth club? *Fraser*
2 Do you feel like going?
3 Sure! Thanks. I'll see you there.
4 Sorry. I have to say no.
5 Would you like to come?
6 That sounds like fun, but I'm sorry, I can't.

6 **Read the phrases for inviting, and accepting and declining invitations.**

Inviting

Do you want to …?
Would you like to …?
Do you feel like … *-ing*?

Accepting

That's a great idea. I'd love to!
Sure! Thanks. I'll see you there.

Declining

That sounds like fun, but I'm sorry, I can't.
Sorry. I have to say no.

7 **Listen to the conversations. Who accepts the invitation? Who declines it? Act out the conversations.**
1.33

Archie Do you feel like [1] going to the movies later?
Fraser That sounds like fun, but I'm sorry, I can't. I have [2] too much homework.

Holly Hello. Would you like to [1] play computer games at my house on Friday night?
Fraser Sorry. I have to say no. [2] My mom's birthday dinner is on Friday.

Yasmin Hi! Do you want to [1] go to a rock concert with me tonight?
Holly That's a great idea. I'd love to!

Archie Do you feel like [1] having lunch at my house on Saturday?
Yasmin Sure! Thanks. I'll see you there.

8 **Work in pairs. Replace the words in purple in Exercise 7. Use these words and/or your own ideas. Act out the conversations.**

1 meet(ing) in the park / go(ing) out for a pizza / see(ing) a horror movie

2 my guitar lesson / my cousin's party

Grammar • Present perfect continuous

How long has she been planning her party?
She has been planning her party for months.
She hasn't been planning her party for very long.

Grammar reference Workbook page 90

1 **Study the grammar table. Choose the correct options to complete the rules.**

1 We form the Present perfect continuous with *have* (or *has*) + *been* + verb + *-ing* / *-ed*.
2 We use this tense for a *short and sudden* / *longer* action that started in the past and *continues* / *doesn't continue* until the present.
3 The action *might* / *won't* continue in the future.

2 **Complete the sentences with the Present perfect continuous form of the verbs in parentheses.**

1 How long *has she been standing* (she/stand) there?
2 I .... (not have) a good time at my new school.
3 He's sweating because he .... (run) for two hours.
4 .... (he/do) homework this morning?
5 They .... (not learn) French for very long.
6 She's very upset. She .... (cry) for 20 minutes.
7 There's a horrible smell in the kitchen! What .... (you/cook)?
8 He's shivering because he .... (swim), and the water's very cold.

3 **Complete the sentences. Use the Present perfect continuous.**

1 I'm really good at English now. I .... .
2 There's green paint in your hair. What .... ?
3 They're very tired. They .... .
4 Your sister's awesome at soccer. How long .... ?
5 This is such a long car trip! We .... .
6 He doesn't know many people in this town because he .... .
7 She's talking to Max on the phone. They .... .
8 We've been in the library. We .... .

Reading

1 Read the article quickly. Which person:

1 was a famous singer? *James*
2 had a celebrity boyfriend?
3 is happy to stay in the background?
4 misses his/her fame?

Most young people dream of being famous, and with all the reality shows and talent contests on TV, it has never been easier to achieve that dream. But does fame bring happiness?

Melanie Greening

I was in a successful reality show when I was eighteen, and I got a job as a TV host after that. My boyfriend was a famous soccer player, and we were in the newspapers all the time. We went to the coolest parties. Life was fantastic! But I wasn't very good at hosting TV shows. I lost my job, and then my boyfriend left me. One month I was a star, and the next I was a nobody. No one recognized me in the street anymore. People have such short memories! It wasn't easy to find another job because I didn't finish high school. I've been working in a clothing store for the last nine months. It's OK, but I was definitely happier when I was famous.

James Levy

I won a TV singing contest when I was sixteen. I was thrilled, but that didn't last long. I was so busy with recording sessions, TV appearances, concerts and photo shoots that I never had time to relax. I really missed my family. They lived far away, so I couldn't see them very often. And the fans were a problem, too. Every time I went out, people used to scream because they were excited to see me. They put their arms around me for a photo, or pushed a pen into my hand so I could sign something for them. One sent me a poisonous spider as a birthday present! Now I write songs, and other people sing them. I still love the music industry. But fame? No, thanks. I prefer a more peaceful life.

Key Words

talent contest	TV host
recognize	recording session
TV appearance	photo shoot

2 (1.34) Read the article again. Are the statements true (T), false (F) or don't know (DK)?

1 Melanie worked for a newspaper. *F*
2 She earned a lot of money when she was famous.
3 People forgot Melanie very quickly after she lost her job.
4 She didn't do well at school.
5 After James won the contest, he had too much free time.
6 He wanted to see his family more often.
7 It was hard to make new friends when he was famous.
8 He enjoyed all the attention from his fans.

Listening

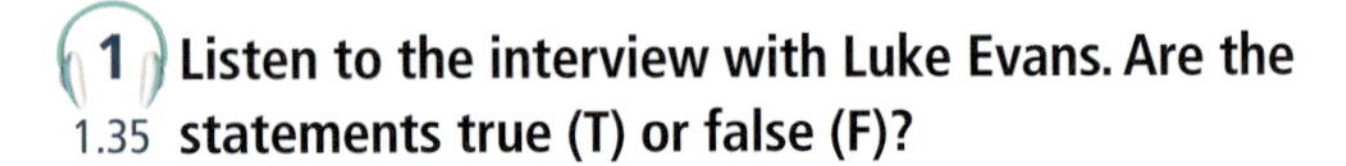

1 (1.35) Listen to the interview with Luke Evans. Are the statements true (T) or false (F)?

1 Luke is an actor.
2 He has been famous since he was five.
3 He's had a crazy life.

Listening Bank Unit 3 page 118

2 In pairs, ask and answer.

1 Do you know about the lives of any child stars?
2 Do you think child stars are lucky? Why?/Why not?
3 Would you like to be famous? Why?/Why not?

Writing • A "for and against" essay

1 **Read the Writing File.**

Writing File Linking words: addition and contrast

You can introduce additional ideas with *and*, *also*, *too* and *additionally*.

I was in a talent contest and I won.
He's an actor. He's also a TV host.
They can sing. They can dance, too.
She's very beautiful. Additionally, she's a very good actor.

You can introduce contrasting ideas with *but*, *however* and *on the other hand*.

She's a nurse, but she wants to be a singer.
He's learning to dance. However, he's not good at it.
Famous singers often come from poor families. On the other hand, a number of singers have wealthy parents.

2 **Answer the questions.**

1 Which words go at the beginning of a sentence?
2 Which word goes after the first or second word in a sentence?
3 Which words go in the middle of a sentence?
4 Which word goes at the end of a sentence?

3 **Complete the sentences with a word or phrase from the Writing File.**

1 My brother's a baseball player. My boyfriend's *also* a baseball player.
2 I like rap music. .... , I don't like jazz.
3 He's been practicing all day, and he's going to practice this evening, ...
4 Living in a city has some advantages. .... , there are some disadvantages.
5 I'm happy to help, ... I don't have much time.
6 Child stars have an exciting life. .... , they earn a lot of money.
7 Robert Pattinson was in one of the Harry Potter movies, ... then he was in the *Twilight* movies.

4 **Read the essay. Find the linking words.**

Wealth Makes People Happy

Many people dream of being rich, but does wealth make people happy?

Rich people certainly don't have the same worries as poor people. They can easily pay for a comfortable home and enough food. They have more choices than ordinary people, too. For example, they don't have to have a job. They can also afford designer clothes and exciting vacations.

On the other hand, good relationships with friends and family are more important than clothes and vacations. It's difficult to know if your friends are genuine if you are rich. Perhaps they are pretending to like you to get some of your money. Additionally, expensive things soon seem ordinary if you can buy them all the time.

In conclusion, rich people definitely have a happier life than very poor people. However, I don't think rich people are always truly happy. The happiest people are in the middle—neither rich nor poor.

5 **Read the essay again and complete the notes.**

Advantages of being rich
They can pay for [1]*a comfortable home* and [2] .... .
They don't have to have [3] .... .
They can afford [4] .... and [5] .... .
Disadvantages of being rich
They don't know if their friends are [6] .... .
Expensive things seem [7] .... to them.
Conclusion
The [8] .... people are not rich and not poor.

6 **You are going to write an essay with the title *Fame Makes People Happy*. Take notes on the advantages and disadvantages of being famous.**

7 **Write your essay. Use the notes in Exercise 5 and the structure of the essay in Exercise 4 to help you.**

Remember!
- Use linking words.
- Use the vocabulary in this unit.
- Check your grammar, spelling and punctuation.

Refresh Your Memory!

Grammar • Review

1 Choose the correct options.

1 I'm lucky *having* / *to have* friends who live near my house.
2 I want *watching* / *to watch* a horror movie at home tonight.
3 Stop *being* / *to be* so rude.
4 She went there *helping* / *to help* her cousin.
5 They were pretending *not recognizing* / *not to recognize* me.
6 *Living* / *To live* at the beach is a lot of fun.
7 We're talking about *going* / *to go* on summer vacation together.

2 Complete the sentences with the correct form of the verbs.

1 It's impossible *to surf* (surf) when there aren't any waves.
2 I'm going to Miami .... (learn) English.
3 He apologized for .... (forget) my birthday.
4 I hate .... (not have) a cell phone.
5 Remember .... (not get) home late tonight.
6 She insisted on .... (pay) for everyone's tickets.
7 He isn't planning .... (finish) school next year.
8 .... (laugh) is the quickest way to feel happier.

3 Complete the conversation with the Present perfect continuous form of the verbs.

A Oh, Jack, there you are! Mom [1] *has been looking* (look) for you. She [2] .... (shout) your name for about ten minutes.
B Oh, sorry. I didn't hear. I [3] .... (listen) to music in the backyard.
A What else [4] .... (you/do) out there? Your hands are red. [5] .... (you/use) red paint?
B No. I [6] .... (not paint). I [7] .... (talk) to Carrie, and we [8] .... (eat) strawberries.
A Well, wash your hands and find Mom. She [9] .... (work) all day, and she's tired. She needs your help.

Vocabulary • Review

4 Complete the sentences with these words.

blushed	cried	gasped
~~laughed~~	shivered	yawned

1 Everyone *laughed* at his joke.
2 She .... in amazement when she heard the news.
3 I .... when I walked out into the snow.
4 She .... for days when her boyfriend left her.
5 I .... when I saw the embarrassing photo.
6 He .... . It was late, and he was tired.

5 Complete the text with the adjective form of the words.

Most of us want to become [1] *wealthy* and live in a big, [2] .... house, but it isn't easy to get rich. [3] .... actors are rich, but most actors are never [4] .... . You could start a business, but it isn't a [5] .... life. It's better not to want a lot of money. If you are [6] .... , live in a place that isn't [7] .... and have good friends and enough food, you are a [8] .... person.

WEALTH
BEAUTY
FAME
SUCCESS
PEACE
HEALTH
DANGER
LUCK

Speaking • Review

6 Make questions and answers. Then listen and check. 1.36

1 **A** you / feel like / go / to the park / ?
Do you feel like going to the park?
B I / be / sorry / I / can't
2 **A** you / like / come / to my house / ?
B great idea / love to / !
3 **A** you / want / meet / downtown / later / ?
B Sorry / have / say no

Dictation

7 Listen and write in your notebook. 1.37

My assessment profile: Workbook page 129

Global Citizenship File

Operation Smile

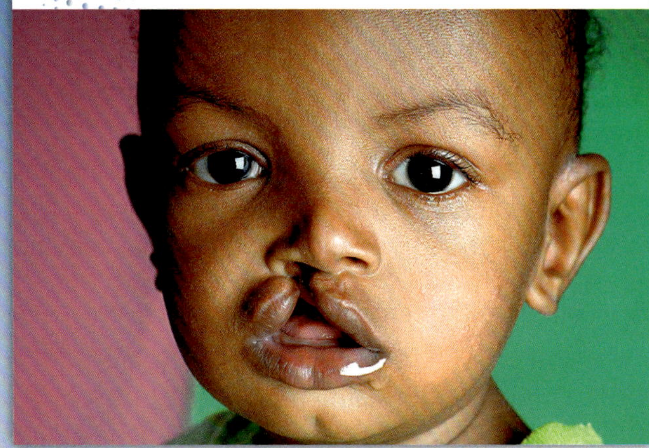

Every three minutes, a child is born with a cleft lip or cleft palate. Children with these conditions have terrible problems with eating, drinking and speaking, and one in ten of them dies before the age of one. The luckier ones live, but they are often rejected by friends and sometimes even by their own families.

In rich countries, simple surgical operations can correct most of these mouth problems and allow children to live normal lives. But in poorer countries, the operations are too expensive for most people, and not enough surgeons are available to do them.

In 1982 Bill Magee, an American doctor, and his wife Kathy, a nurse, went to the Philippines to do some cleft palate surgeries. But it was a short trip, and there wasn't time to help all the children who needed surgery. They felt terribly guilty. When they got home, they started a new charity. They called it Operation Smile.

Operation Smile now works in more than sixty countries. Five thousand volunteers give their time and skills to provide free mouth surgery to the children who need it most. The charity also provides medical equipment and trains local doctors to do the surgery themselves. In this way, the results of an Operation Smile visit continue long into the future.

When an international group of doctors and nurses travels to a country, two high school students go, too. The students usually have done a lot of fundraising in their local area and told a lot of people about the work of Operation Smile. Their trip is a fantastic way to experience a completely different culture and help to change lives forever.

Reading

1 Read the article quickly. Are the statements true (T) or false (F)?

1 Operation Smile is a charity. *T*
2 It helps children with medical problems.
3 Most of its work is in the US.
4 All its volunteers are doctors and nurses.

2 Read the article again and answer the questions. 1.38

1 Why are cleft lips and cleft palates dangerous?
Because children can have terrible problems with eating, drinking and speaking.
2 Why is it difficult to have these operations in some countries?
3 Why did the Magees start Operation Smile?
4 What three things does Operation Smile do?
5 How can students go on an Operation Smile trip?

3 Listen to the interview. Copy and complete the report. 1.39

Name	*Marisa Correa*
Country visited	....
Length of trip	.... days
Work	Taught children and parents about staying .... and taking care of .... .
Enjoyed trip?	Yes / No
Number of operations	....

My Global Citizenship File

4 Find out about another important charity that teenagers can help. Answer these questions.

- What work does it do?
- Why is its work important?
- What can teenagers do to help?
- What do teenagers say about their experiences with the charity?

5 Make a poster for the charity, advertising for teenage volunteers.

Grammar • Past simple/Past continuous

1 Choose the correct options.

Yesterday I [1] *visited / was visiting* my cousins in New Haven. When I [2] *arrived / was arriving* at their house, they [3] *listened / were listening* to music in their room. We [4] *didn't have / weren't having* lunch at their house. We [5] *took / were taking* the bus to Church Street. While we [6] *ate / were eating* lunch at the diner, we [7] *saw / were seeing* the actor Claire Danes.

2 Make sentences.

1 We / walk to school / when / my sister / drop / her camera on the ground
We were walking to school when my sister dropped her camera on the ground.
2 While / Bob / talk on the phone / he / hear / a loud noise outside
3 My friends / play Frisbee / in the park / when / it / start / to rain
4 Nina / sprain / her ankle / while / she / run / in the backyard
5 My brother / see / a robbery / while / he / work / in the supermarket

• Used to

3 Look at the notes. Make sentences about what people used to do and didn't use to do in the 1980s.

In the 1980s

✗	✓
send emails	send faxes
watch DVDs	watch videos
have cell phones	use public pay phones
use computers at home	use typewriters

In the 1980s, people didn't use to send emails; they used to send faxes.

• Present perfect + *ever, never, already, yet*

4 Choose the correct options.

1 I've *never / ever* eaten Japanese food.
2 Have you eaten your lunch *yet / ever*?
3 I've *already / never* cleaned up my room, but I haven't walked the dog *yet / already*.
4 This is the funniest joke I've *ever / already* heard!

5 Complete the sentences with *for* or *since*.

1 We've lived in this house *for* six years.
2 Greg's had the same bike .... 2012.
3 .... she was a child, Nora's been a fan of basketball.
4 I haven't seen Adam .... a while! Is he OK?

6 Complete the sentences. Use the Present perfect.

1 *Have* you *ever met* (ever/meet) a famous person?
2 My mother .... (never fly) in a plane.
3 **A** Do you want a sandwich?
B No, thanks. I .... (already/eat) lunch.
4 .... you .... this book .... ? (read/yet)

• Present perfect/Past simple

7 Make questions in the Present perfect and answers in the Past simple.

1 you / ever / win a prize?
yes / win / singing contest / two years ago
Have you ever won a prize?
Yes. I won a singing contest two years ago.
2 you / see / the new James Bond movie?
yes / see / it / last weekend
3 your parents / buy / a new car?
yes / buy / a Volkswagen / on Saturday
4 Peter / lose / his new phone?
yes / lose / it / at the party last night

8 Complete the text with the Present perfect or Past simple form of the verbs.

My sister [1] *'s already come* (already/come) back from France. She [2] .... (go) there on vacation with her friends, Jenny and Sarah. They [3] .... (stay) in a hotel in Paris. I [4] .... (never/visit) France, but I [5] .... (just/read) a really interesting book about the Eiffel Tower.

• Gerunds and infinitives

9 Choose the correct options.

1 It's difficult *to review / reviewing* for exams in the summer because I like *to be / being* outside with my friends, and I don't want *to read / reading* books in my room.
2 I used my new camera *to take / taking* this photo of my dog. He was trying *to catch / catching* a rabbit.
3 It's important not *to get / getting* angry when you can't do something. Remember *to try / trying* hard, and don't be afraid of *to fail / failing*.

10 Complete the text with the infinitive or gerund form of the verbs.

I hope [1] *to spend* (spend) the summer at the beach. I love [2] .... (swim), and I also enjoy [3] .... (play) beach volleyball. My brother, however, prefers [4] .... (go) on activity vacations. He's decided [5] .... (travel) with our cousin this summer. They're planning [6] .... (take) the train to Scotland and then go mountain climbing.

• Present perfect continuous

11 Make questions and answers in the Present perfect continuous.

1 How long / you / wait / here
I / wait / here / for half an hour
How long have you been waiting here?
I've been waiting here for half an hour.
2 How long / your sister / learn / Chinese
She / learn / Chinese / since 2011
3 How long / Jess and Emma / work / at this café
They / work / at this café / for three months
4 How long / we / stand / on this platform
We / stand / on this platform / for 40 minutes

12 Complete the text with the Present perfect continuous form of the verbs.

I just got my black belt in judo! I [1] *'ve been practicing* (practice) martial arts for ten years, but I [2] .... (not/study) judo for very long. My dad [3] .... (teach) judo since 2007. My friends [4] .... (come) to his classes with me recently, and we [5] .... (watch) martial arts movies together afterward.

Speaking • Expressing extremes

1 Complete the conversation with these words.

really amazing	really awful	~~so good~~
such a great	such a terrible	

A Your brother's very talented. He's [1] *so good* at music.
B Yes, he's written some [2] .... songs.
A And he's [3] .... pianist as well.
B That's true. But he's a [4] .... singer.
A I didn't know that!
B Yes, he has [5] .... voice!
A Oh no!

• Giving/Responding to news

2 Complete the conversation.

A [1] *What's up,* Dan?
B I [2] j.... h.... the most incredible news.
A What [3] h.... ?
B You won't [4] b.... it, but my brother has won the regional under-16 diving competition.
A You're [5] k.... m.... !
B [6] S.... . My mom just called me. He's made it to the national finals!

• Invitations

3 Put the conversation in the correct order.

☐ a That sounds like fun, but I'm sorry, I can't. I have a tennis lesson this afternoon.
☐ b Do you want to meet me at the corner store on Hill Street at 6 o'clock? Then we can buy some popcorn and eat it at home while we're watching the movie.
☐ c That's a great idea. I'd love to!
☐ d Sure. Thanks. I'll see you there.
1 e Hi, Katie. Do you feel like going to the park this afternoon?
☐ f Oh well, would you like to come to my house later this evening? We can watch a DVD.

Vocabulary • Compound nouns

1 Complete the compound nouns in the sentences.

1 My father used to be a *business* person in the city, but now he works as a ....fighter in a small town.
2 When we went to New York, we saw a lot of sky.... .
3 The speed.... was racing through the water when the pilot saw the light.... .
4 We traveled fast through the snow on our snow.... .
5 My ....mates and I copied the information about our ....work from the white.... .
6 My little sister goes to a baby.... after school because my parents work until 6 p.m.
7 That isn't a space.... in the sky—it's a balloon!
8 The old wind.... just outside our town still makes flour for the local baker.

• Phrasal verbs 1

2 Choose the correct options.

1 My friends often hang *out* / *off* at the mall on the weekend, but I can't—my mom counts *on* / *of* me to watch my little brother.
2 You have to fill *up* / *out* this form before you set *out* / *up* your own business.
3 I'm looking *for* / *about* my cat. He ran *away* / *out* yesterday.
4 I give *away* / *up*! I want to find *up* / *out* some information for my geography project, but my computer isn't working.
5 When we get *before* / *back* from vacation, I will go *out* / *up* with my friends.

• Collocations with *make, go* and *keep*

3 Find the word or phrase that doesn't fit.

1 keep *a secret* / *together* / *control*
2 make *crazy* / *a difference* / *it to the finals*
3 keep *calm* / *a difference* / *in touch*
4 go *for a walk* / *a dream come true* / *out*
5 make *in touch* / *someone's dream come true* / *a decision*
6 go *crazy* / *together* / *control*

• Jobs and suffixes *-or, -er, -ist*

4 Copy the table and complete the list.

things	jobs
art	*artist*
....	novelist
....	photographer
play	....
poem	....
....	sculptor

• Showing feelings

5 Complete the sentences with the correct form of these verbs.

~~blush~~ frown gasp laugh scream
shiver smile sweat yawn

1 She was embarrassed, so she *blushed*.
2 The girl .... loudly at my joke.
3 He's very tired. He's .... .
4 When it's hot, we .... , and when it's cold, we .... .
5 She .... with surprise when the door opened and then .... in terror when she saw the ghost.
6 He is .... because he's in a bad mood at the moment, but when he's happy, he always .... .

• Adjective suffixes

6 Put the letters in the correct order to complete the adjectives.

1 u b i a e t — *beauti*ful
2 e l h h a t — _ _ _ _ _ _ y
3 a m f — _ _ _ ous
4 e a w h l t — _ _ _ _ _ _ y
5 s n o i p o — _ _ _ _ _ _ ous
6 k l u c — _ _ _ _ y
7 c s c s e s u — _ _ _ _ _ _ _ ful
8 c p a e e — _ _ _ _ _ ful
9 g d a n e r — _ _ _ _ _ _ ous

Word list

Unit 1 • Different Lives

Compound nouns

babysitter	/ˈbeɪbiˌsɪtɚ/
business person	/ˈbɪznɪsˈ ˌpɚsən/
classmate	/ˈklæsmeɪt/
firefighter	/ˈfaɪɚˌfaɪt̬ ɚ/
homework	/ˈhoʊmwɚk/
lighthouse	/ˈlaɪthaʊs/
skyscraper	/ˈskaɪˌskreɪpɚ/
snowmobile	/ˈsnoʊmoʊˌbil/
spaceship	/ˈspeɪsˌʃɪp/
speedboat	/ˈspidboʊt/
whiteboard	/ˈwaɪtbɔrd/
windmill	/ˈwɪndˌmɪl/

Phrasal verbs

count on	/ˈkaʊnt ɔn/
fill out	/ˌfɪl ˈaʊt/
find out	/ˌfaɪnd ˈaʊt/
get back	/ˌgɛt ˈbæk/
give up	/ˌgɪv ˈʌp/
go out	/ˌgo ˈaʊt/
hang out	/ˌhæŋ ˈaʊt/
look for	/ˌlʊk ˈfɔr/
run away	/ˌrʌn əˈweɪ/
set up	/ˌsɛt ˈʌp/

Unit 2 • Aiming High

Collocations with *make, go* and *keep*

go crazy	/ˌgoʊ ˈkreɪzi/
go for a walk	/ˌgoʊ fɚ ə ‘wɔk/
go together	/ˌgoʊ təˈgɛðɚ/
go well	/ˌgoʊ ˈwɛl/
keep a secret	/ˌkip ə ˈsikrɪt/
keep calm	/ˌkip ˈkɑm/
keep control	/ˌkip kənˈtroʊl/
keep in touch	/ˌkip ɪn ˈtʌtʃ/
make a decision	/ˌmeɪk ə dɪˈsɪʒən/
make a difference	/ˌmeɪk ə ˈdɪfrəns/
make it to the finals	/ˌmeɪk ɪt tə ðə ˈfaɪnəlz/
make someone's dream come true	/ˌmeɪk ˈsʌmwʌnz ˌdrim ˈkʌm ˈtru/

Jobs and suffixes *-or, -er, -ist*

Common stative verbs (see page 12)

be	believe	belong	cost	feel
get	hate	have	hear	know
like	love	need	own	see
smell	taste	think	understand	want

art	/ɑrt/
artist	/ˈɑrt̬ ɪst/
novel	/ˈnɑvəl/
novelist	/ˈnɑvəlɪst/
photograph	/ˈfoʊt̬ əˌgræf/
photographer	/fəˈtɑgrəfɚ/
play	/pleɪ/
playwright	/ˈpleɪraɪt/
poem	/ˈpoʊəm/
poet	/ˈpoʊɪt/
sculptor	/ˈskʌlptɚ/
sculpture	/ˈskʌlptʃɚ/

Unit 3 • Be Happy!

Showing feelings

blush	/blʌʃ/
cry	/kraɪ/
frown	/fraʊn/
gasp	/gæsp/
laugh	/læf/
scream	/skrim/
shiver	/ˈʃɪvɚ/
shout	/ʃaʊt/
sigh	/saɪ/
smile	/smaɪl/
sweat	/swɛt/
yawn	/yɔn/

Adjective suffixes

beautiful	/ˈbyut̬ əfəl/
dangerous	/ˈdeɪndʒərəs/
famous	/ˈfeɪməs/
healthy	/ˈhɛlθi/
lucky	/ˈlʌki/
peaceful	/ˈpisfəl/
poisonous	/ˈpɔɪzənəs/
successful	/səkˈsɛsfəl/
wealthy	/ˈwɛlθi/

4 Survive!

Grammar
Modals: ability, obligation, prohibition, advice, possibility; Past modals

Vocabulary
Natural disasters; Phrasal verbs 2

Speaking
Asking for clarification

Writing
Giving instructions

Word list page 77
Workbook page 107

Vocabulary • Natural disasters

1 2.1 **Match sentences (1–9) to photos (a–i). Then listen, check and repeat.**

1 When **volcanoes erupt**, they are dangerous. *i*
2 **Earthquakes** can **destroy** buildings.
3 People sometimes **drown** in **floods**.
4 A **disease** can **spread** very quickly.
5 In a **famine**, people sometimes **starve**.
6 An **avalanche** can **bury** you under snow.
7 Most plants can't **survive** in a **drought**.
8 A **hurricane** is a storm with very strong winds.
9 A **tsunami** is a huge, dangerous wave.

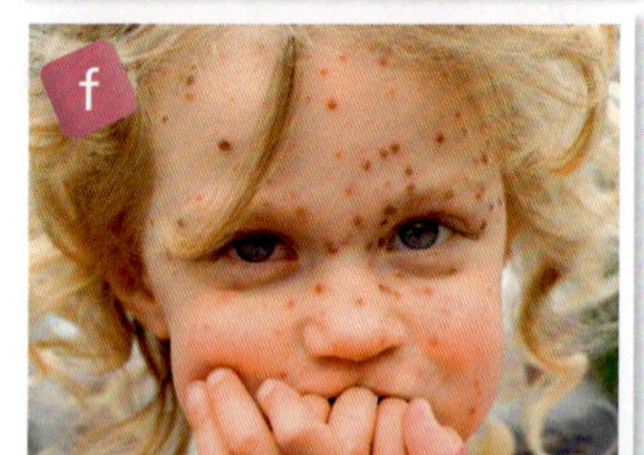

2 2.2 **Complete the sentences with the correct form of the words in bold in Exercise 1. Then listen and check.**

1 In the story of Noah's Ark, there was a great *flood*.
2 Mount Vesuvius is a .... that .... in AD 79 and .... the Roman city of Pompeii under five meters of ash.
3 A lot of people .... on the *Titanic* in 1912. Wealthy passengers were more likely to .... .
4 60,000 men died in an .... in the Alps in World War I.
5 6,000,000 people .... in a .... in Ukraine in the 1930s.
6 The world's longest .... was in the Atacama Desert in Chile. It didn't rain there for 400 years.
7 An .... near the coast of Japan in 2011 caused a terrible .... . The disaster killed more than 15,000 people and .... more than 300,000 buildings.
8 .... Katrina devastated New Orleans in 2005.
9 Malaria is a .... that mosquitoes .... .

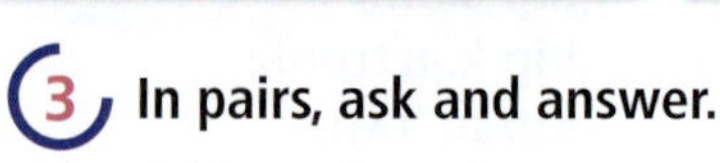

3 **In pairs, ask and answer.**

1 Have there been any natural disasters in your country? What happened?
2 What natural disasters have happened in other countries? What can you remember about them?

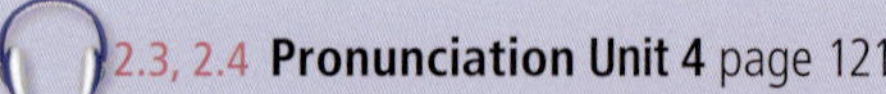
2.3, 2.4 **Pronunciation Unit 4** page 121

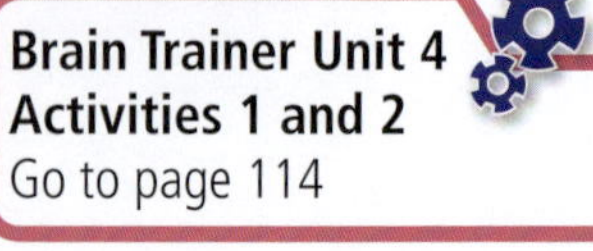
Brain Trainer Unit 4
Activities 1 and 2
Go to page 114

Reading

1 Look at the photos. Answer the questions.

1 What part of the world do you think this is?
2 What bad news does the article give?
3 What good news does it give?

2 Read the article quickly and check your answers.

3 Match sentences (1–4) to blanks (A–D) in the article.

1 It came in 2007.
2 Not everyone in Bangladesh was so lucky.
3 It was one of the worst natural disasters of the twentieth century.
4 "You must come to the school now," they shouted.

4 2.5 **Read the article again. Are the statements true (T) or false (F)?**

1 Because of global warming, there are more natural disasters now than there were in the past. *T*
2 The cyclone in 1991 was stronger than the cyclone in 1970.
3 The cyclone in 1991 killed more people than the cyclone in 1970.
4 In 1991 there was nowhere safe for women and children to go.
5 A scientist in the US helped to save lives in Cyclone Sidr.
6 The buildings in Rupa's village survived because of the cyclone warning.

5 What about you? In pairs, ask and answer.

1 Are there ever floods in your country? What problems do they cause?
2 What do people do to prepare for natural disasters in your country? Do you think they do enough?
3 Many charities say "There are more floods and droughts now because of global warming. Rich countries should pay the poor countries affected by these problems." Why do they say this? Do you agree? Why?/Why not?

Fighting Disasters

Every year, natural disasters affect about 250 million people. Global warming is making droughts, floods and avalanches more common. We can't stop the disasters, but we can reduce the number of people who die in them.

In Bangladesh, a lot of people have to live on flat land near the ocean, but strong winds, called cyclones in this part of the world, bring terrible floods. In 1970 Cyclone Bhola killed about 500,000 people. **A** .... In 1991 the even stronger Cyclone Gorky hit the country. This time, people could use special school buildings as emergency shelters. Unfortunately, many women and children didn't go to them, and around 140,000 people drowned.

After this, villages set up groups of emergency volunteers, and teachers had to talk to children every week about the things they should do if there was a cyclone warning.

They didn't have to wait many years for the next big cyclone. **B** *1* Twelve hours before Cyclone Sidr reached land, a Bangladeshi scientist in the US used a computer to calculate the exact areas of danger. The emergency volunteers in the villages spread the warning fast.

Ten-year-old Rupa Begum and her friends ran to all their neighbors' homes. **C** .... "You won't be safe if you stay here." All the buildings in the village were destroyed in the disaster, except for the school shelter. Thanks to the children's warnings, everyone in the village survived.

D .... Four thousand people died in Cyclone Sidr. But this was a much smaller number than in the big cyclones of the twentieth century. With modern technology, planning and education, we don't have to lose huge numbers of lives in natural disasters.

Grammar • Modals: ability, obligation, prohibition, advice

Ability
We can reduce the number of people who die.
We can't stop natural disasters.
Obligation
You must come to the school now.
They have to live on flat land near the ocean.
We don't have to lose huge numbers of lives.
Prohibition
You mustn't leave the shelter.
Advice
You should listen to the warnings.
You shouldn't go near the ocean.

Grammar reference Workbook page 92

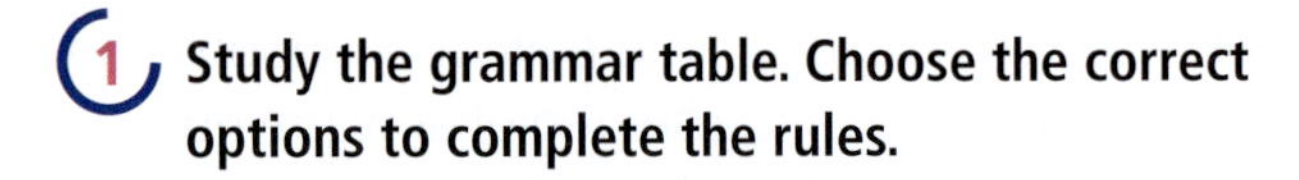

1 Study the grammar table. Choose the correct options to complete the rules.

1 We use *must* or *have to* when an action is *necessary / against the rules.*
2 We use *don't have to* when an action is *impossible for someone / not necessary.*
3 We use *should* when an action is *a good idea / impossible for someone.*
4 We use *can* when an action is *not necessary / possible* for someone.
5 We use *mustn't* when an action is *a good idea / against the rules.*

2 Choose the correct options.

1 The mountains are popular because people *can / must* ski and climb there.
2 You *have to / mustn't* do mountain sports alone.
3 You *should / can't* check the weather before you go into the mountains.
4 People *must / shouldn't* go on the snow when there's a danger of avalanches.
5 If you are buried in an avalanche, you *don't have to / can't* get out. The snow is too heavy.
6 You *have to / don't have to* wait for help.

3 Choose the correct option, A, B, C or D, to complete the conversation.

Dad You look tired. You [1] *D (should)* go to bed.
Bill I [2] .... go to bed yet. I [3] .... to study French.
Dad Your French test isn't tomorrow; it's on Friday. You [4] .... study tonight. You [5] .... study another day.
Bill No, I [6] .... do it tonight, because I'm busy for the rest of the week. And I [7] .... get a bad grade on in the test.
Dad You [8] .... worry so much. Tonight sleep is more important than the test!

1 **A** shouldn't **B** mustn't **C** can't **D** should
2 **A** can **B** should **C** can't **D** must
3 **A** have **B** must **C** shouldn't **D** can
4 **A** don't have to **B** mustn't **C** can't **D** don't have
5 **A** mustn't **B** can **C** doesn't have to **D** can't
6 **A** must **B** mustn't **C** don't have **D** have
7 **A** should **B** must **C** mustn't **D** have to
8 **A** should **B** must **C** shouldn't **D** can

4 Make sentences. Change the underlined words. Use these words.

can don't have to has to must mustn't ~~should~~ shouldn't

1 It's a good idea to get some exercise. (You)
You should get some exercise.
2 I have to call Lucy. (I)
3 It isn't necessary to pay for the food. (You)
4 It's against the rules to use our cell phones in class. (We)
5 It's a bad idea to eat a lot of candy. (People)
6 She's free to go shopping on Saturday. (She)

5 What about you? Discuss in pairs.

1 rules at your school
2 rules at home
3 advice for someone who is new at your school

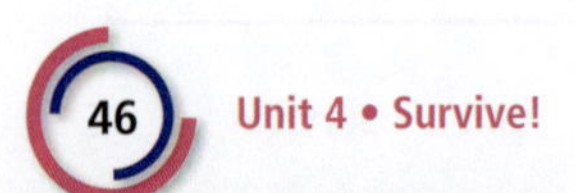

• Past modals

People could use schools as shelters.
I couldn't speak English when I was six.
They had to teach children about the dangers.
They didn't have to wait long for the next cyclone.

Grammar reference Workbook page 92

Watch Out!
We can't use *must* for obligation in the past.

6 **Study the grammar table. Complete the rules.**

1 For ability in the past, we use .... / .... .
2 For obligation in the past, we use .... / .... .

7 **Change these sentences to the past tense.**

1 She can't swim.
She couldn't swim.
2 Can you see the avalanche?
3 They don't have to help us.
4 He must be careful.

Vocabulary • Phrasal verbs 2

1 2.6 **Read the text. Complete the phrasal verbs (1–10) and match them to their definitions (a–j). Then listen, check and repeat.**

1 break *down*
2 calm ....
3 come ....
4 figure ....
5 get ....
6 keep ....
7 look ....
8 put ....
9 run ....
10 take ....

a continue
b get dressed in something
c stop wearing something
d stop worrying
e stop working or functioning *1*
f come to the end of a difficult time
g be excited about something that's going to happen
h use all of something, so there isn't any more of it
i meet without planning to
j calculate or understand

Word list page 77 **Workbook** page 107

My Journal

I was looking forward to the sailing race, but after only three days of racing, the wind disappeared. Then my engine broke down, and the radio stopped working. I kept on trying to fix it, but I couldn't figure out what was wrong with it. The sun was very strong, so I took off my T-shirt and put it on my head. But then, while I was working on the engine, I fell and broke my leg. I was running out of drinking water, too. Could I get through this alive? Finally, I calmed down and waited quietly. After 24 hours, a boat came across mine and helped me to safety.

2 **Complete the sentences with the correct form of the words from Exercise 1.**

1 Stop screaming and *calm down*! We won't .... this if we don't think sensibly.
2 The car didn't .... . It .... gas.
3 .... looking at the map, and you'll .... our location soon.
4 I'm really .... the weekend. I'm going to Maine.
5 .... your dirty clothes, and .... some clean ones!
6 Today I .... an online ad for a volcano tour.

3 **Work in pairs. Choose six phrasal verbs from Exercise 1 and write a short conversation with them.**

Brain Trainer Unit 4 Activity 3
Go to page 114

Chatroom Asking for clarification

Speaking and Listening

1 **Look at the photo. Answer the questions.**

1 Where are Archie, Holly and Yasmin?
2 What do you think just happened to Holly?
3 Who do you think Yasmin is talking to?

2 **Listen and read the conversation. Check your answers.** 2.7

3 **Listen and read again. Answer the questions.** 2.7

1 What is wrong with Holly's foot?
A snake bit it.
2 Does it hurt?
3 Is Archie worried about Holly? Why?/Why not?
4 Is an ambulance going to come?
5 Where does Holly have to go later?

4 **Act out the conversation in groups of three.**

Archie Hurry up, guys!
Holly We're coming … Ouch! What was that?
Yasmin Oh no! A snake! Did it bite you?
Holly Yes, on my foot.
Yasmin Poor thing! That must really hurt!
Holly Yes, and it could be really dangerous …
Archie Calm down, Holly. It might be a poisonous snake, but it probably isn't deadly. There aren't that many deadly snakes in here.
Yasmin I'll call the doctor. *(on phone)* Hello, my friend has a snake bite on her foot. What should we do? … Sorry, I don't understand. What do you mean? Are you saying that we should call for an ambulance, or keep on walking? … Oh, I see! Thanks.
Holly What does the doctor think?
Yasmin You have to go to the hospital. But we don't have to call an ambulance, so it can't be too serious.

Say it in your language …
Hurry up!
Ouch!

5 Look back at the conversation. Complete these sentences.

1 Sorry, I don't *understand*.
2 What do you .... ?
3 Are you .... that we should call for an ambulance, or keep on walking?
4 Oh, ... ! Thanks.

6 Read the phrases for asking for clarification.

Asking for clarification

What do you mean?
Sorry, I don't understand.
Are you saying that ...?
Oh, I see! Thanks.

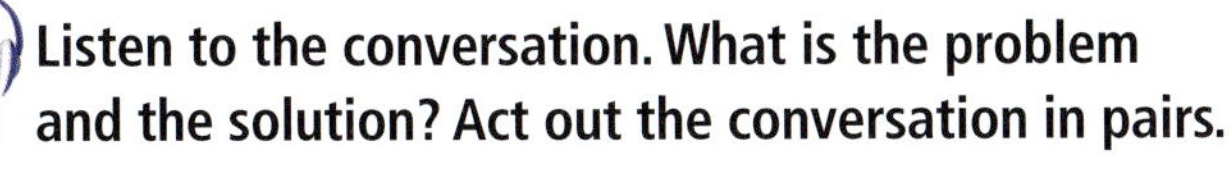

7 Listen to the conversation. What is the problem and the solution? Act out the conversation in pairs.

2.8

Archie You shouldn't [1] swim in that river because of the [2] water.
Yasmin Sorry, I don't understand. Are you saying that [3] the water is dangerous?
Archie Yes. So you shouldn't [4] swim in it.
Yasmin What do you mean?
Archie Well, [5] people have caught diseases here. You should [6] swim in a swimming pool.
Yasmin Oh, I see! Thanks.

8 Work in pairs. Replace the words in purple in Exercise 7. Use these words and/or your own ideas. Act out the conversations.

You shouldn't ski there because of the snow.

Sorry, I don't ...

1 ski there / visit that volcano / keep food in your tent
2 snow / gas / bears
3 there's a problem with the snow / gas is coming from the volcano / there are bears around here
4 ski on it today / go there / keep food in your tent
5 there are often avalanches here / the gas is poisonous / bears steal food from tents
6 ski somewhere else / visit a different place / leave it in the campsite kitchen

Grammar • Modals: possibility

That bite must hurt.
It might be a poisonous snake.
The bite could be really dangerous.
The snake can't be deadly.

Grammar reference Workbook page 92

1 Read the grammar table. Complete the rules.

1 When something is possible, we use .... or .... .
2 When something is impossible, we use .... .
3 When something is certain, we use .... .

2 Choose the correct options.

A Where's Jackie?
B She isn't here. She [1] *could* / *must* be in her tent, or she [2] *might* / *can't* be down by the river.
A She [3] *must* / *can't* be in her tent. It's empty.
B Listen! Someone's yelling from the river. That [4] *must* / *can't* be her.
A She isn't yelling, she's screaming. She [5] *must* / *could* be scared!
B You're right. She [6] *might* / *can't* be in danger! Let's go and help her.

3 Make two sentences for each picture. Use *must*, *might*, *could* or *can't*.

1 Who is this? Jason and Luke both like surfing.
It might be Jason.
It could be Luke.

2 Where is this volcano? There aren't any volcanoes in Maryland, but there are some in Oregon.

3 What animal is that? Dolphins are gray, and sharks are gray, too.

Reading

1 **Look at the photo and the title of the article. How do you think a television show saved this boy's life?**

Teenager Jake Denham was skiing with his family in the US when he fell and lost one of his skis. His family didn't know that he had a problem. They kept on skiing. When they got to the bottom of the mountain, there was no sign of Jake.

Jake couldn't find his ski anywhere. In the end, he decided to take off his other ski and walk down the mountain. But he couldn't figure out the right way to go.

It was now getting dark, and he was a long way from any shelter. He knew that he might die that night in the cold temperatures. But Jake kept calm. At home, Jake watched a lot of TV shows about surviving in difficult situations. He remembered the advice from these shows and knew that he should build a cave in the snow. He made a hole and pointed it up the hill so the wind couldn't blow into it. Outside his cave, the temperature fell to a dangerous -15°C that night, but inside it Jake was safe from the cold.

But he had to get down the mountain. The TV shows always said, "If you are lost, you should find someone else's tracks through the snow and follow them." "I wanted to live my life," remembers Jake. "So I got up, and I found some ski tracks, and I followed those." He walked and walked, and finally he saw lights. Nine hours after he lost his ski, he came across a team of rescue workers. He was safe!

His mom was so relieved when she heard the news! Amazingly, Jake didn't even have to go to the hospital. He got through the ordeal without any injuries.

So, the next time someone says that watching TV is a waste of time, think of Jake. Sometimes TV can save your life!

Key Words

cave	hole	blow
track	rescue	ordeal

2 **Read the article quickly and check your answer to Exercise 1.**

3 (2.9) **Read the article again and put these events in the correct order. Which event didn't happen?**

a He sheltered in a snow cave.
b He found rescuers.
c He fell. *1*
d He went to the hospital.
e He got lost.
f He followed ski tracks.

4 (2.9) **Read the article again. Answer the questions.**

1 Why didn't Jake's family help him when he fell?
Because they didn't know he had a problem, and they kept on skiing.
2 At first, what did Jake plan to do?
3 Why was it dangerous for Jake when it got dark?
4 Why was his snow cave a good design?
5 How long was Jake lost on the mountain?
6 What injuries did Jake have?

Listening

1 (2.10) **Listen to a mountain rescue worker talk about survival shows on TV. Are the statements true (T) or false (F)?**

1 They can help people.
2 They can give people dangerous ideas.
3 People should copy all the things that they see on survival shows.

Listening Bank Unit 4 page 119

2 **In pairs, discuss the questions. Give reasons.**

1 Do you ever watch survival shows on TV? Do you enjoy them?
2 Do you think the advice on survival shows is useful?
3 Imagine yourself in a dangerous situation like Jake's. Do you think you would survive?

Writing • Giving instructions

1 Read the Writing File.

Writing File Giving clear instructions

Use headings so people can find the right information quickly.

- **Use bullet points.**
- **Keep sentences short.**
- **Don't use linking words at the beginning of sentences.**

2 Read the information pamphlet. How many bullet points are there? How many sentences are there in the longest bullet points?

HOW TO Survive an Earthquake

Be prepared

- If the danger of earthquakes is high in your area, find out about organizations that can send free earthquake warnings by text message. You might have a few seconds before the earthquake reaches you. A few seconds could save your life.

Before or during an earthquake

- People inside buildings should hide under a sturdy table or desk, away from windows and heavy objects on walls.
- If you are cooking, turn off the gas or electricity.
- People in outside areas should move away from buildings, trees and power lines.
- Drivers should drive carefully away from bridges, buildings, trees and power lines, and then stop their car. They shouldn't leave the car.

After an earthquake

- In areas near the ocean, tsunamis sometimes develop after earthquakes. You should listen to the radio. If there is any danger of a tsunami in your area, run to high ground.

3 Match the headings (1–3) to the advice (a–c).

1 Avoid the problem
2 Reduce the danger
3 During an attack

a Never swim in waters where there have been recent shark attacks.
b Hit the shark hard in the eyes or the end of its nose.
c Wear dark clothes. To a shark, people in bright colors might look like fish.

4 You are going to write an information pamphlet about survival in the desert, or your own idea. Look at the ideas in the pictures and/or do your own research. Take some notes.

5 Write your information pamphlet. Use your notes from Exercise 4.

Remember!
- Use headings and bullet points.
- Use the vocabulary in this unit.
- Check your grammar, spelling and punctuation.

Refresh Your Memory!

Grammar • Review

1 Choose the correct options.

1 Rabbits *can't / must* fly.
2 You *could / mustn't* forget your book. You'll need it.
3 Last year I *must / had to* learn Chinese. It was really difficult.
4 I've been learning English for seven years, so I *can / have to* speak it pretty well now.
5 You *should / mustn't* try harder in class.
6 My mom *can't / couldn't* swim when she was a child.
7 You *mustn't / don't have to* wash your hair every day. Twice a week is enough.
8 We *had to / could* see the ocean from the house where we stayed last summer.
9 She *mustn't / should* forget her hockey stick today because she's playing in a game.
10 I *have to / can't* study tonight because we have an important test tomorrow.
11 You *can / shouldn't* swim in the lake. It's very dangerous.
12 My grandpa *mustn't / didn't have to* study science at school.

2 Complete the sentences with these verbs. Sometimes more than one answer is possible.

can't	could	might	must

1 He *must* like chocolate. Everyone likes chocolate!
2 She .... live in Costa Rica. I'm not sure.
3 I lost my bag. It .... be somewhere at school, or maybe at Tom's house.
4 He .... have a sister who's 30. His mom and dad are only 40.
5 They .... be from France. They don't speak any French.
6 The people near the erupting volcano .... feel very scared.
7 That car .... cost a lot of money. It's a BMW, and BMWs are always expensive.
8 She .... play the piano. I don't know.

Vocabulary • Review

3 Complete the sentences.

1 A *volcano* often produces ash when it e.... .
2 A.... happen in the mountains. If they b.... you in snow, it's very difficult to s.... .
3 If it doesn't rain for weeks, there's a d.... , and it can lead to a f.... . Many people s.... .
4 A h.... is a very strong wind that can d.... houses.
5 A serious d.... can s.... among people very quickly.
6 T.... are big waves after an e.... out in the ocean. They cause terrible f.... , and a lot of people d.... .

4 Complete the sentences with these words.

~~across~~	down (x2)	forward	of	off
on (x2)	out (x2)	through	to	

1 I came *across* Lia in town yesterday.
2 Put .... a sun hat. It'll protect you from sunburn.
3 We've run .... milk. I'll go and buy some more.
4 Calm .... . It's not the end of the world.
5 We're really looking .... our vacation.
6 She figured .... a way to cross the river safely.
7 I was late because our car broke .... .
8 Don't worry! You'll get .... the exams OK.
9 Take .... your sweater if you're too hot.
10 He kept .... walking until he found help.

Speaking • Review

5 Complete the conversation with these words. Then listen and check. 2.11

Are you saying	I don't understand.
I see!	~~What do you mean?~~

A We don't have to go to school tomorrow.
B [1] *What do you mean?* It's Monday tomorrow.
A Yes, but there's no school when there's a flood.
B Sorry, [2] .... [3] .... that there's a flood at school?
A Yes, there is. There's water in the classrooms.
B Oh, [4] .... Thanks for telling me.

Dictation

6 Listen and write in your notebook. 2.12

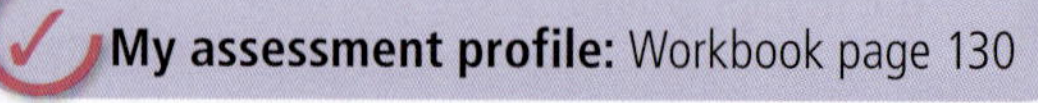

My assessment profile: Workbook page 130

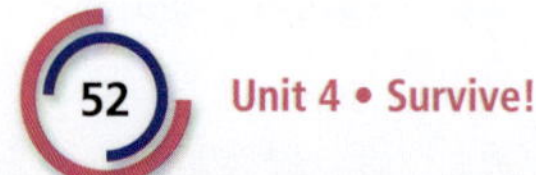

Real World Profiles

Richard Turere's Profile

Age	Home country
13	Kenya

My favorite things …
helping my family, inventing things

Reading

1 Read Richard's profile and look at the photos. How do you think he helped his family? Read the article quickly to check.

2 Read the article again. Answer the questions. 2.13

1 Why are lions a good thing for Kenya?
Because they attract hundreds of thousands of tourists every year.
2 Why do farmers kill them?
3 How many lions are there in Kenya?
4 Why couldn't Richard's farm have a fence to keep out the lions?
5 Why did his "lion lights" keep the lions away?
6 Was it expensive to make the lights?
7 What two groups did his lights help?
8 How has Richard's life changed since people heard about his lights?

Lion Lights

Lions are important to the people of Kenya because they attract hundreds of thousands of tourists every year. However, they also kill a lot of farm animals. In a country where droughts are common, it's hard for farmers to feed their families. It isn't surprising that they sometimes kill lions to protect their farms.

Twenty years ago, there were 10,000 lions in Kenya. Now there are only 2,000. Conservationists started to think that there was no hope for the lions' future. But then they heard about Richard Turere.

From the age of nine, it was Richard's job to take care of his family's cows. But when lions came out of the forest at night and ate them, Richard could do nothing. A fence high enough and strong enough to keep the lions out was too expensive.

When he was eleven, Richard realized that the lions never attacked when someone was moving around outside with a flashlight. They were afraid of humans. This gave Richard an idea. Maybe he could design some lights that could trick the lions. With an old car battery, a solar panel and some bulbs from broken flashlights, he created outside lights that looked like a moving flashlight. Since then, the lions have never come back to his farm.

Soon his neighbors asked him to put up "lion lights" at their farms, too. Again, the lights worked perfectly. Conservationists were very excited! Here was something simple and cheap that could both help farmers to feed their families and help the lions to survive.

And there was help for Richard, too. One of Kenya's best schools heard about his clever invention and offered him a free education there. Richard now hopes to become an engineer and invent many other useful things in the future.

Class discussion

1 What do you think is more important, the lions or the farmers' animals? Why?
2 Do you know of any other simple ideas to keep unwanted animals away?
3 What did you have to do when you were eleven? Compare your life at that age with Richard's life.

5 Work for It

Grammar
Will/Going to; Present simple/Present continuous for future

Vocabulary
Work collocations; Job qualities

Speaking
Phone language

Writing
An email about plans

Word list page 77
Workbook page 108

Vocabulary • Work collocations

1 2.14 **Match the items in the picture (1–11) to these words. One word is missing from the picture. Then listen, check and repeat.**

appointments
copies
email
front desk
inquiry
meeting
office supplies
payments
phone
presentation *1*
report
spreadsheet

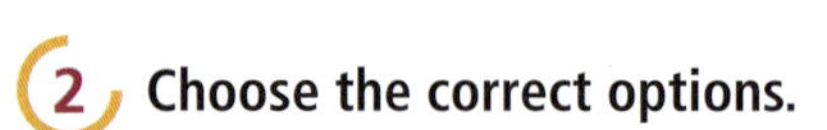

2 Choose the correct options.

1 attend *a meeting* / *a spreadsheet*
2 answer *an appointment* / *the phone*
3 deal *at the front desk* / *with inquiries*
4 write *a meeting* / *a report*
5 give *inquiries* / *a presentation*
6 make *an appointment* / *a phone*
7 check *emails* / *a meeting*
8 work *some copies* / *at the front desk*
9 prepare *a spreadsheet* / *at the front desk*
10 take *an appointment* / *payments*
11 make *some copies* / *a meeting*
12 order *office supplies* / *inquiries*

2.15, 2.16 **Pronunciation Unit 5** page 121

3 2.17 **Listen to Dan and Julie. What did they do yesterday? Use the collocations from Exercise 2.**

Dan worked at the front desk; …
Julie …

4 Work in pairs. What do you think these people do at work? Use the words in Exercise 2 to help you.

- a secretary
- a teacher
- a police officer
- a salesperson
- a mechanic

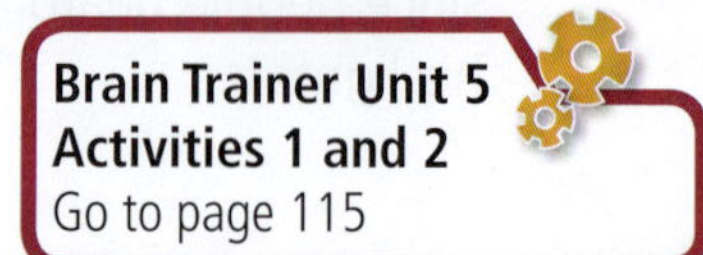
Brain Trainer Unit 5
Activities 1 and 2
Go to page 115

Reading

1 Read the webpage quickly. Choose the best description.

1 It describes different job opportunities for young people when they leave school.
2 It advises students on how to apply for a job.
3 It describes a way to get work experience before leaving school.

2 (2.18) Read the webpage again. Are the statements true (T), false (F) or don't know (DK)?

1 Alleghany High School students do a semester of work experience. *T*
2 Rema is still in school.
3 Jed didn't like the people at the building supplies company.
4 Babblefish wants to be a math teacher.
5 Clarkson is good at repairing vehicles.
6 Clarkson isn't looking forward to going out on a test drive.
7 Batgirl is going to help with teaching sports on her placement.
8 She probably won't use the phone during her week at the gym.

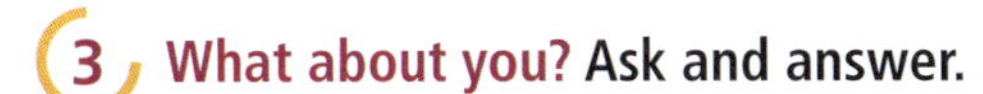

3 What about you? Ask and answer.

1 Have you done any part-time jobs or had any work experience?
2 What kind of work would be interesting/useful as work experience for you?

Work Experience

Today we're looking at work experience. Juniors and seniors at Alleghany High School in Virginia can do a semester of work experience. It's a great chance to find out about the skills you will need for the world of work.

Rema did her work experience at a local cell phone store and loved it! When she left school, she applied for a job there, and now she's the area manager.

Jed got a work placement with a building supplies company. He prepared some spreadsheets for the sales team, attended a marketing meeting and made a lot of copies. "Some of the work was boring," said Jed, "but the people were great."

COMMENTS

Tell us about your plans. What are you going to do for your work experience?

I'm going to spend a week at an elementary school because I want to be a teacher. I'm going to observe some math classes and accompany the children on a field trip to a farm. I'll probably be very tired by the end of the week, but I'm really looking forward to it. **BABBLEFISH**

I have a placement with the Police Vehicle Workshop, where mechanics repair police cars. I love trying to understand how vehicles and machines work, so I think this placement will be really interesting. I'm going to help the mechanics, wash and clean the cars and, best of all, I'm going to go out on some test drives with the mechanics! **CLARKSON**

I love sports, especially tennis, so I got a work placement at my local gym. I'm going to assist with beginners' tennis coaching and organize the sports equipment. I'll probably also work at the front desk, make appointments for gym training sessions, take payments and deal with telephone inquiries. **BATGIRL**

Grammar • Will/Going to

will
Are you thirsty? I'll get you a drink.
I'll probably be very tired by the end of the week.

going to
I'm going to spend a week at an elementary school.
The chair is broken. You're going to fall!

Grammar reference Workbook page 94

1 **Study the grammar table. Match the beginnings (1–2) to the endings (a–d) of the sentences to complete the rules.**

1 We use *will*
2 We use *going to*

a to make predictions about the future.
b to talk about plans and intentions.
c to express sudden decisions.
d to make a prediction when we have some evidence.

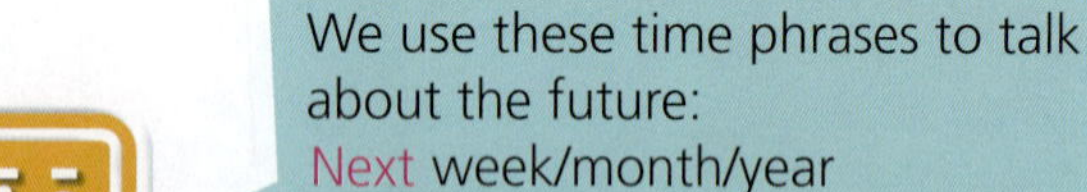

Watch Out!
We use these time phrases to talk about the future:
Next week/month/year
In three days
By Tuesday/the weekend/the end of the month
In the next week/month/year

2 **Match the statements and questions (1–6) to the sentences (a–f).**

1 I started my new job today. *d*
2 What are your vacation plans?
3 We missed the bus.
4 We don't have any bread.
5 Do you want to watch a DVD at my house?
6 I'm sorry, I can't meet you later.

a I'll go to the store and get some.
b That's a great idea. I'll bring some popcorn.
c We're going to be late.
d I think I'll really enjoy it.
e I'm going to visit my grandmother in the hospital.
f We're going to visit San Francisco.

3 **Choose the correct options, *will* or *going to*.**

1 Next year I'*ll* / '*m going to* study physics.
2 You're driving too fast! Look at the car in front of you! You'*ll* / '*re going to* crash!
3 **A** Do you want a ham or a cheese sandwich?
B I'*ll* / '*m going to* have a cheese sandwich.
4 I think you'*ll* / '*re going to* be a millionaire before you're 25.
5 *Is your brother going to* / *Will your brother* play in the baseball game tomorrow?

4 **Complete the conversation with the correct form of the verbs.**

A Hi, Ben. I just put the kettle on. Do you want tea or coffee?
B Thanks, Mom. I [1] *'ll have* (have) a coffee, please.
A [2] .... (you/see) Uncle Joe this afternoon?
B No, I [3] .... (be). I [4] .... (play) tennis with Jen. Why?
A Oh, I want to return this book to him.
B Well, I [5] .... (take) it to his house after tennis.
A Are you sure about tennis? Look at the clouds! It [6] .... . (rain)
B You're right. Jen [7] .... (probably/cancel) the game. I [8] .... (call) her now.

5 **Work in pairs. Write two true statements and two false statements about your weekend plans. Can your partner guess the false statements?**

A I'm going to play tennis with my cousin.
B True!
A Yes. I'm going to bake a chocolate cake.
B False!
A No, it's true.

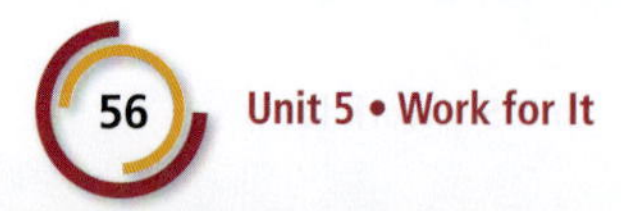

Vocabulary • Job qualities

1 2.19 **Look at these words and phrases. Check the meanings in a dictionary. Then listen and repeat.**

accurate	analytical	excellent IT skills
experienced	good communicator	leadership qualities
organized	~~patient~~	practical
punctual	reliable	team player

Word list page 77
Workbook page 108

2 Complete the sentences with the words from Exercise 1.

1 A *patient* person stays calm and is prepared to wait if necessary.
2 An .... person is efficient and is good at planning his/her time.
3 A .... can express himself/herself well and can give information in a clear way.
4 A .... person is never late.
5 A person with .... is good at being the most important person in a group and likes making decisions.
6 An .... person looks at information carefully and finds the important facts and figures.
7 A .... person likes doing active, useful work.
8 A .... works well with other people and thinks about all the people in his/her group.
9 An .... person has already done a similar job.
10 A .... person is someone you can trust and believe.
11 A person with .... is good at using computers.
12 An .... person is very careful with his/her work and hardly ever makes mistakes.

3 Work in pairs. Use words and phrases from Exercise 1 to complete the job advertisements.

Editorial Manager

We are looking for a person with [1] *leadership qualities* to be the manager of a team of six. The ideal candidate will be [2] .... and has worked in publishing for at least five years. We need a [3] .... who can give clear and interesting presentations to large groups of people.

Veterinary Assistant

Our large, friendly Vet's Surgery is looking for a [4].... person who can help our vets with everyday work. It's important to be [5].... , as we open at 8:30 every morning, and our ideal candidate will also have [6].... and can update our spreadsheets.

School Receptionist

We are looking for a [7] .... person who can stay calm and won't panic in our busy office. We want an [8] .... person who can plan meetings and keep our reports and files in order. Our ideal School Receptionist will be a [9] .... who can work together with a large group of teachers and school administrators.

Data Analyst

Our statistics department has a vacancy for an [10] .... worker to look at health data and collect statistics. We need [11] .... information, with no mistakes. The Data Analyst works with important and confidential information, and we want a [12] .... person for the job.

4 What about you? In pairs, ask and answer.

1 Tell your partner about a time in your life when you achieved something or did something really well.
2 Which qualities does this achievement show?

Brain Trainer Unit 5 Activity 3
Go to page 115

Chatroom Phone language

Speaking and Listening

1 Look at the photo. What is Archie doing? Does Holly look interested or bored?

2 Read and listen to the conversation. Check your answers. 2.20

3 Listen and read again. Answer the questions. 2.20

1 What does Holly ask Archie to look for? *a job in the paper*
2 What is the name of the store?
3 Who is Judy?
4 Why can't Holly go to the store tomorrow morning?
5 What should Holly take with her to the store?

4 Act out the conversation in groups of four.

Holly	Are there any jobs in the paper?
Archie	Here's one. "Clothing store needs reliable salesperson for Saturday afternoons."
Holly	That sounds perfect! I'll call them now …
Man	Hello, Fashion Fix.
Holly	Oh, hello. I'm calling about the salesperson job. Can I speak to the manager?
Man	You need to speak to Judy, but she just went out. Can I take a message?
Holly	Yes, please. My name's Holly Brightman, and I'm 16 years old. My number is …
Man	Hold on. She just came in. I'll put her on. Just a moment.
Judy	Hello, Holly. What are you doing tomorrow?
Holly	I have a tennis lesson in the morning, but it ends at 12 o'clock. After that, I'm not doing anything.
Judy	Well, let's talk at the store tomorrow afternoon. Bring your résumé!
Holly	Fantastic! I can't wait!

Say it in your language …

That sounds perfect!

I can't wait!

5 **Look back at the conversation. Find these expressions.**

1 Two ways to say: *Wait a minute.* *Hold on.*
2 One way to say: *You can talk to her now.*
3 One way to say: *The reason for my call is …*

6 **Read the phrases about phone language.**

Saying who you are and why you're calling
My name's …/It's …
I'm calling about …
I'd like to/Can I speak to …?
Asking someone to wait
Just a moment.
Hold on, please.
Transferring a call
I'll transfer you now.
I'll put him/her on.
Offering to take a message
Can I take a message?

7 2.21 **Listen to the conversation. Act out the conversation in pairs.**

Receptionist Hello. [1] Penney's Sports Club.
Yasmin Oh, hello. Can I speak to [2] Mr. Ryder, please?
Receptionist I'm sorry, he's [3] not here at the moment. Can I take a message?
Yasmin Yes, please. My name's [4] Yasmin Hayes. I'm calling about the [5] badminton lessons.
Receptionist Oh, he just came back. I'll transfer you now.
Yasmin Thank you.

8 **Work in pairs. Replace the words in purple in Exercise 7. Use these words and/or your own ideas. Act out the conversations.**

1 Pizza Delight / iMart Stores / Hills Garden Center
2 Sarah Morgan / the manager / Ms. Thorne
3 busy / just went out / talking to a customer
4 [your name]
5 job in the kitchen / cashier job / salesperson job

Grammar • Present simple and Present continuous for future

Present simple	Present continuous
The train leaves at 5 o'clock. My tennis lesson ends at 12.	What are you doing tomorrow? I'm meeting my friend for lunch.

Grammar reference Workbook page 94

1 **Study the grammar table. Choose the correct options to complete the rules.**

1 We use the *Present simple / Present continuous* for arrangements.
2 We use the *Present simple / Present continuous* for scheduled events.

2 **Choose the correct options.**

A [1] *What do you do / What are you doing* on the weekend?
B [2] *We visit / We're visiting* our friends in New Orleans, Louisiana.
A [3] *Do you fly / Are you flying* there?
B Yes, we [4] *do / are*. The flight [5] *departs / is departing* Atlanta at 7 a.m. on Saturday.
A That's early! What time [6] *does it arrive / is it arriving* in New Orleans?
B It [7] *gets / is getting* to New Orleans at 8:30.

3 **Complete the sentences with the Present simple or Present continuous form of these verbs.**

drive have open sing ~~start~~ study

1 Our English exam *starts* at 4 o'clock.
2 The new clothing store .... this afternoon at two o'clock.
3 We .... to our aunt's house tomorrow.
4 My brother .... languages at college in September.
5 I .... a guitar lesson tomorrow after lunch.
6 I .... in a talent contest on Sunday.

4 **Invent some exciting plans for tomorrow. Include two definite events. Work in pairs. Tell your partner about your plans.**

I'm meeting Robert Pattinson tomorrow evening. We're attending a movie premiere and …

Reading

1 **Read the article quickly. Choose the best headline.**

1 How to Choose Your Perfect Career
2 Jobs of the Future?
3 The World of Science Fiction

Nadia checks her watch and jumps into her jet car. Her heli-bus leaves at ten o'clock, and she doesn't want to be late. She's starting her new job today with AstroStar Flights, as a tour guide around space. Sound like a page from a science-fiction book? Well, maybe the jet car and the heli-bus are closer to science fiction than to reality, but the job of space tour guide will probably exist by the year 2020. Virgin Galactic is already taking reservations for its space flights, and although a ticket today costs $200,000, space flights will probably get much cheaper in the near future.

Experts believe that some current jobs—for example, call center workers, or supermarket cashiers—will soon become unnecessary because machines will gradually replace people. But there will be other new and exciting jobs in our world of the future. Are you organized, practical and good at paying attention to detail? Then perhaps in 2020 you will be a robot mechanic and maintain and repair the thousands of robots that we will use in our home and working life.

Perhaps you're a great communicator and love talking to people? In the future, online friendships will become as important as real-life friendships, and companies will employ social media managers to maintain their online profiles. If you like working with animals, and you care about the environment, then migration manager might be a good job for you. Migration managers will help to move endangered animals from dangerous habitats to new homes.

But of course, if you're analytical and like looking at statistics and making predictions, then there's already a perfect job for you. You can become a futurologist and predict how our world will develop over the next 20, 30 or 50 years.

Key Words

reality	reservation
social media	endangered
habitat	develop

2 2.22 **Read the article again. Answer these questions.**

1 Does the job of space tour guide exist now?
No, it doesn't.
2 How much does a ticket on a Virgin Galactic flight cost?
3 What qualities will a robot mechanic need to have?
4 Why will companies employ social media managers in the future?
5 What will migration managers do?
6 What kind of person might enjoy the job of a futurologist?

Listening

1 2.23 **Listen to the conversation. Where is Tom going to work?**

a on a boat
b on a ride at a theme park
c in a restaurant

Listening Bank Unit 5 page 119

2 **Discuss the questions.**

1 Would you like to work at a theme park? Why?/Why not?
2 What's your ideal summer job?
3 Can you think of any other unusual summer jobs for teenagers?

Writing • An email about plans

1 **Read the Writing File.**

Writing File Expressing degrees of certainty

We can use adverbs of certainty to express how sure we are about a future event.

100% sure ↓ *certainly, definitely*
probably
maybe, perhaps

certainly, definitely, probably

These adverbs go

- **before** the main verb.
  He definitely lives here.
- **between** the auxiliary and the main verb.
  I'm probably taking a taxi to the airport.
- **after** the verb *to be*.
  She's certainly good at math. Look at her test score!

maybe, perhaps

These adverbs often go at the beginning of the sentence.

- Maybe we'll move to Hawaii next year.
- Perhaps Sarah isn't feeling well.

I think …

We can also use *I think* + subject + verb.

- I think she'll call tomorrow. (but I'm not certain)

2 **Make sentences.**

1 visit / in / will / We / our / probably / cousins / Kansas City
We will probably visit our cousins in Kansas City.
2 sister / Maybe / party / your / to / come / the / won't / tomorrow
3 in / definitely / is / Your / closet / bag / the
4 apply / I / for / think / job / I'll / this
5 close / lives / Our / probably / the / to / school / teacher
6 they're / Perhaps / by / traveling / bus

3 **Read the email and find the expressions of certainty.**

New Message

Hi Judy,

How are you? Are you looking forward to the weekend? I have a lot of plans for this weekend. I'm probably going to go swimming with friends on Saturday morning, and then I think we'll have lunch at this new diner near the park.

In the afternoon, my sister and I are taking the train to New York because we have tickets for a Kings of Leon concert at Madison Square Garden! I'm a big fan! I don't know when we'll get back, but my dad will definitely meet us at the station, since it's usually very late.

Maybe we'll go to the park on Sunday morning, but I think I'll be too tired after Saturday night. In the afternoon, we're having a big barbecue. I think the weather will be OK (the forecast is good). I'm going to finish my history project on Sunday evening … my history teacher is probably collecting all the finished projects on Monday morning!

What are you doing this weekend? Tell me about your plans!

Rachel xx

SEND

4 **Read the email again and answer the questions.**

1 What is Rachel probably going to do before lunch on Saturday? *go swimming with friends*
2 Where is she probably going to have lunch on Saturday?
3 Why are Rachel and her sister traveling to New York on Saturday afternoon?
4 Why is Rachel's dad meeting her at the station on Saturday night?
5 When is Rachel going to finish her history project?

5 **You are going to write a reply to Rachel. You can use your real plans for the weekend, or you can make them up. Think about these questions.**

- Are you going to hang out with friends?
- What will the weather be like?
- Are you going to play any sports or music?
- Are you going to travel anywhere? If so, how will you get there?

6 **Now write your reply. Use your ideas from Exercise 5.**

Remember!

- Use expressions of degrees of certainty.
- Use the vocabulary in this unit.
- Check your grammar, spelling and punctuation.

Refresh Your Memory!

Grammar • Review

1 Complete the conversation with *going to* or *will* and the verbs in parentheses.

A ¹ *Are you going to go* (you/go) to the basketball game this afternoon?
B Yes, I ² .... (be). And then I ³ .... (meet) Hailey at the Parrot café.
A Actually, the café's closed this week.
B Then maybe we ⁴ .... (try) the new place in the park.
A I think you ⁵ .... (like) it! The pastries there are delicious.
B I ⁶ .... (buy) one for you there, then.
A Oh, thank you! And don't forget your umbrella! I just saw the weather forecast. It ⁷ .... (rain) later today.
B Well, maybe we ⁸ .... (not go) to the place in the park after all.

2 Make sentences. Use the correct form of the verbs.

1 I / take the train / to New Haven / tomorrow
I'm taking the train to New Haven tomorrow.
2 The train / leave / at 9:30
3 It / arrive in New Haven / at 11:15
4 I / meet / my friends / at the Franklin Theater
5 We / appear / in a comedy show
6 The show / start / at 12 o'clock
7 It / not finish / until 3:30
8 After the show / we / go / to a party

3 Choose the correct options to complete the text.

I ¹ *'m starting* / *will start* my new job at a clothing store in Washington, DC, tomorrow. I'm really excited! I ² *'m going to get up* / *get up* very early because I don't want to be late on my first day. My train ³ *'s going to leave* / *leaves* at 7:30, and my sister ⁴ *will* / *is going to* drive me to the station. I think I ⁵ *will* / *am going to* enjoy the job because I love fashion, and the store has some beautiful clothes. After work I ⁶ *will meet* / *'m meeting* some friends at a diner near the station. We ⁷ *are having* / *are going to have* a meal together, and I ⁸ *tell* / *will tell* them all about my new job.

Vocabulary • Review

4 Complete the collocations with these words.

answer	attend	check	deal	give	make (x2)
order	prepare	take	work	~~write~~	

1 *write* a report
2 .... a meeting
3 .... some copies
4 .... payments
5 .... office supplies
6 .... with inquiries
7 .... at the front desk
8 .... emails
9 .... a presentation
10 .... the phone
11 .... a spreadsheet
12 .... an appointment

5 Complete the sentences with the correct job qualities.

1 Mary is good at working with groups of people, and she is never late.
She's a t*eam* p*laye*r and is p*unctua*l.
2 Harry has done this job for ten years, and he is good with computers.
He is e .... d and has e .... t IT s .... s.
3 Jodie never makes mistakes in her work. She always stays calm and doesn't get angry with other people.
She is a .... e and p .... t.

Speaking • Review

6 Put the conversation in the correct order. Then listen and check. 2.24

a I'm sorry, she's out at the moment. Can I take a message?
b Hold on, Adam. She's back now. I'll put her on.
c Oh, hello. Can I speak to the manager, please?
d Yes, please. My name's Adam Barnett. I'm calling about the assistant librarian job.
e Hello, Fulton Library. *1*

Dictation

7 Listen and write in your notebook. 2.25

My assessment profile: Workbook page 131

The Story of Innocent™ Smoothies

Adam Balon, Richard Reed and Jon Wright were friends from college. They all had well-paid jobs, but they also shared a dream. They wanted to start their own company, but they didn't know what *product* to make. They decided to focus on a target *market* that they knew and understood—young people who lived in cities and worked hard. These people wanted to have a healthy lifestyle, but didn't always have the time to prepare healthy food. Adam, Richard and Jon developed some smoothies—fruit juice combined with crushed fruit. But first, they wanted to test their product. So in August 1998, they spent $850 on fruit and sold their smoothies at a local music festival. They hung a big banner over their stand, saying, "Should we quit our jobs to make these smoothies?" Beneath the banner were two trash cans for the empty smoothie bottles, a "Yes" trash can and a "No" trash can.

At the end of the festival, the "Yes" trash can was full of bottles. The friends resigned from their jobs the next day and started up "Innocent Smoothies." Next, they needed some *funding* for their company. They wrote hundreds of letters to possible *investors*, but had no success. However, they kept on trying, and finally Maurice Pinto, a wealthy American, agreed to invest $430,000 in their business.

The rest is history . . . Innocent Smoothies now sells more than two million bottles of smoothies per week, and it employs over 250 people. Why is it so successful? Adam, Richard and Jon weren't experienced *entrepreneurs*, but they were organized and practical, and they believed in their product. The success of Innocent Smoothies in a big corporate world shows how important personality can be in the success of a business.

Reading

1 Read the article quickly. Put the events in the correct order.

a They sold smoothies at a music festival.
b They found a wealthy investor.
c Innocent Smoothies became very successful.
d They quit their jobs.
e Adam, Richard and Jon made smoothies. *1*

2 Read the article again. Find the words in italics that match these definitions.

1 people who set up a business *entrepreneurs*
2 money
3 something that people make and then sell
4 people who give money to a business and then take a share of the profit
5 people who you are selling your product to

3 (2.26) Read the article again. Are the statements true (T) or false (F)?

1 Adam, Richard and Jon were friends in college. *T*
2 Young people who work in cities usually have a healthy lifestyle.
3 Most people at the festival liked the smoothies.
4 Adam, Richard and Jon found an investor easily.
5 Innocent Smoothies is now very successful.

4 (2.27) Listen to the marketing expert and complete the notes.

The marketing mix: The four Ps

1 *Product*: is it right for the market? What makes it 2 .... ?

3 .... : do you want it to be more or less 4 .... than other products?

Promotion: are you going to use 5 .... on TV or in 6 .... ?

7 .... : do you want to sell your product in 8 .... general stores or in 9 .... designer stores?

My Business Studies File

5 Work in small groups. Think about a product that you could make and sell. Discuss these questions.

- Who/What is your target market?
- Are there any similar products on the market?
- How will you find the funding for your business?
- What do you want your product to look like?

6 Prepare a presentation for the class about your business idea. Then give your presentation.

6 Coast

Grammar
Passive statements;
Passive questions

Vocabulary
Coastal life; Word building:
Verbs with prefixes
dis- and *re-*

Speaking
Asking for and giving
directions

Writing
A field trip report

Word list page 77
Workbook page 109

Vocabulary • Coastal life

1 Match the photos (1–12) to these words. Then listen, check and repeat.

2.28

arcade
beach chair
beach umbrella
cliffs
go-carts
harbor
hot dog stand *1*
ice cream stand
pier
seagull
seawall
souvenir shop

1 

2 

3 

4 

5 

6 

7 

8 

9 

10 

11 

12 

2 Complete the texts with words from Exercise 1.

Unread Message

Hi Jon,

This is my last family vacation ever! A [1] *seagull* just ate my sandwich, and I have nothing to do! I want to go to the [2] .... and buy a postcard, but Mom says that I'll spend all my money. Dad won't let me ride the [3] .... because he says they're too fast, and instead they want to visit the boring [4] .... and look at tons of boats!

Oh well—this evening we're going to go to the [5] .... for dinner, and maybe I can even get an ice cream cone from the [6] .... . So it's not all bad.

Sadie

Gina,

Here's a photo of our new white [7] .... . Isn't it lovely? I can sit here on my [8] .... and look out at the ocean—I can even see the tall [9] .... far away. A lot of people visit the [10] .... on the [11] .... , where there are tons of games to play. But I prefer the peace and quiet here.

Hope you're well!

Aunt Helen

3 **What about you?** In pairs, ask and answer.

- Which seaside attractions do you have in your country?
- What do you usually do at the beach?

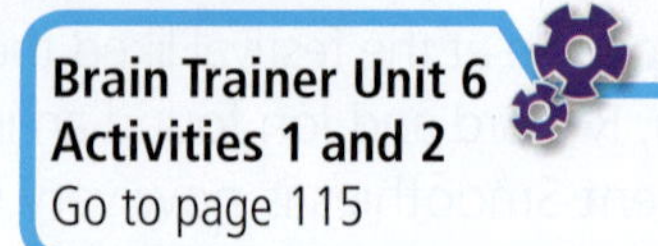

Brain Trainer Unit 6
Activities 1 and 2
Go to page 115

Reading

1 **Match the photos (1–4) to the places (A–B). Read the texts quickly and check your answers.**

2 **Read the texts again. Where can you …**
2.29
1 ride a go-cart? *Ocean City*
2 see penguins and whales?
3 see a working harbor?
4 listen to live music?
5 buy some jewelry?
6 go sea kayaking?

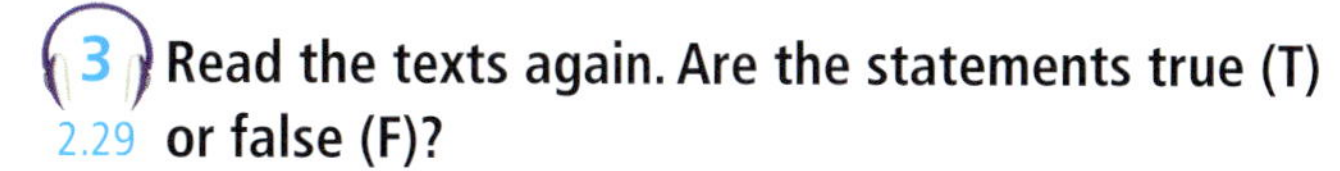

3 **Read the texts again. Are the statements true (T) or false (F)?**
2.29
1 Ocean City is very busy all year round. *F*
2 When the weather is bad, Max and his friends sometimes go to the arcades.
3 Max often goes kite surfing in winter.
4 Kayla probably lives close to the beach.
5 Not many people know about the penguins in Simon's Town.
6 The weather in Simon's Town in winter is better than in many other coastal towns.

4 **In pairs, ask and answer.**
1 Which place in the texts would you prefer to visit on vacation? Why?
2 Which place would you prefer to live in? Why?
3 How does your hometown change in the different seasons?

A

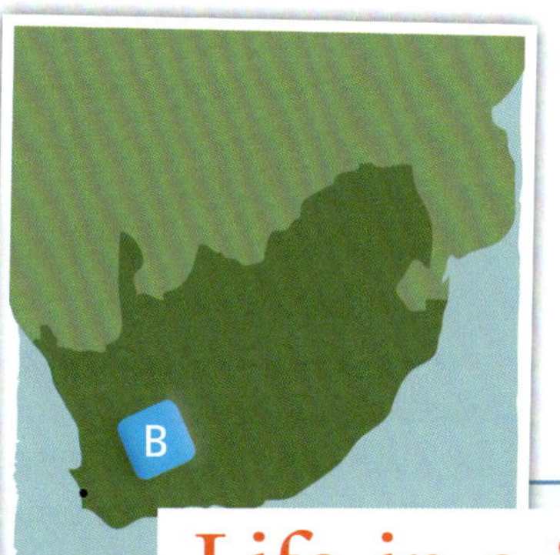

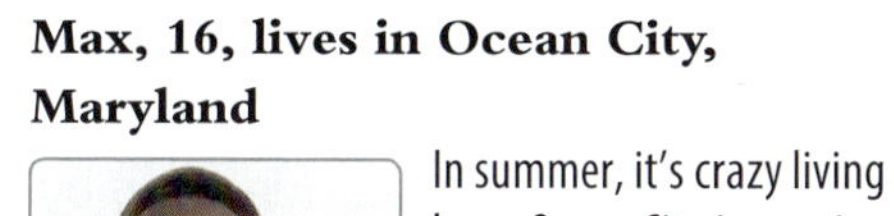

Life in a Seaside Town

Max, 16, lives in Ocean City, Maryland

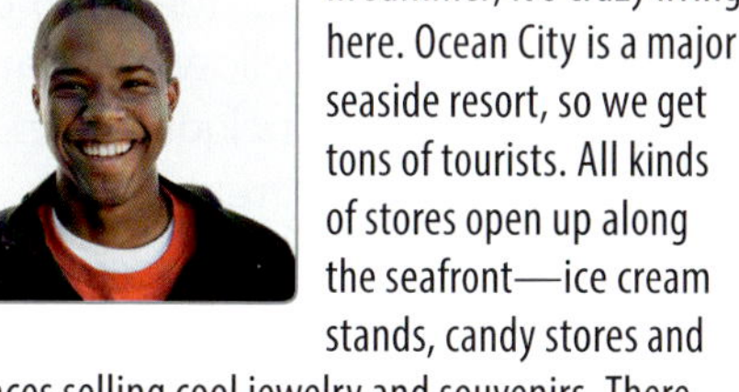

In summer, it's crazy living here. Ocean City is a major seaside resort, so we get tons of tourists. All kinds of stores open up along the seafront—ice cream stands, candy stores and places selling cool jewelry and souvenirs. There are also several amusement parks near the beach, with cool rides and go-cart tracks, and a lot of arcades. My friends and I hang out there sometimes and play video games when the weather is not so good. There are also concerts and sand sculpture exhibitions on the beach in summer. The winter is much quieter, and a lot of the summer stores are closed, but the beaches in Ocean City are perfect for kite surfing from October to March. I don't go often because it's expensive, but it's a lot of fun!

Kayla, 17, lives in Simon's Town, South Africa

The amazing thing about Simon's Town is the wildlife. I can walk to the beach in the morning and see whales out in the ocean, and penguins and otters on the beach. There are more than 3,000 African penguins on Boulders Beach, and a lot of tourists come to Simon's Town just to see them! But Simon's Town is also a naval base, and it has a working harbor, so there are always ships coming in and out of the bay. Most places along the Cape Peninsula are wet and windy in the winter, but we're lucky in Simon's Town because it's protected from the winds and rain by the Cape Peninsula mountains. My friends and I often go hiking in winter, and sometimes we go sea kayaking. The sea is too rough for kayaking in summer, but it's calmer in winter, and we can get really close to the whales and seals!

1

2

3

4

Grammar • Passive statements

The town is protected by the mountains.
The buildings were destroyed by a huge fire.
The work will be finished tomorrow.

Grammar reference Workbook page 96

1 Study the grammar table. Choose the correct options to complete the rules.

1 Passive sentences start with the person or thing that *does the action / the action happens to.*
2 The main verb in passive sentences is always the *infinitive / past participle.*
3 We use *by / from* before the agent (the person who or the thing that does the action).

2 Make these sentences passive.

1 Many people admire the beautiful cottages in Cape Cod, Massachusetts.
The beautiful cottages in Cape Cod, Massachusetts, are admired by many people.
2 The owners completely rebuilt their cottage a few years ago.
The cottage .... .
3 They put a new kitchen with a stove in the cottage.
A new kitchen .... .
4 They bought beautiful furniture for the cottage.
Beautiful furniture .... .
5 The owners sold it in 2012 for $380,000.
It was .... .
6 A rich family with two children bought it.
It .... .

2.30 **Pronunciation Unit 6** page 121

3 Complete the article with the passive form of the verbs.

Sand Sculptures

In 2006, in the seaside town of Weston-super-Mare, in England, an amazing sand sculpture of King Kong [1] *was produced* (produce) by two Dutch sculptors. Twenty tons of sand [2] .... (use) to make the sculpture, and it [3] .... (admire) by thousands of visitors. But unfortunately, the sculpture [4] .... (destroy) by vandals a month later. The following year, sculptures from different fairy tales, including *Cinderella* and *Alice in Wonderland,* [5] .... (create).

The Weston-super-Mare city council is now planning the exhibition for next year. "A new and exciting theme for the exhibition [6] .... (announce) next week," said Councilor Jones.

How to make a sand sculpture

Wet sand [7] .... (use) to make the sand sculptures. Water [8] .... (pour) onto the sand, and then the wet sand [9] .... (press) down to remove all the air. Finally, the sand [10] .... (form) into the right shape.

4 What about you? Work in pairs. Use the verbs in the box to describe one of these processes.

add heat pour stir

- how to make a cup of coffee

cut put slice spread

- how to make a cheese and tomato sandwich

Vocabulary • Verbs with prefixes *dis-* and *re-*

1 2.31 **Match these words to the definitions (1–11). Then listen, check and repeat.**

disagree	disappear *1*	discontinue	discover
dislike	recover	release	remove
replace	research	restore	

1 become lost or impossible to see
2 clean and repair something or give something back to someone
3 take something away
4 stop producing something
5 study a subject in detail
6 become healthy again or bring back something that was lost
7 find
8 have a different opinion than that of another person or people
9 think someone or something is not very nice
10 allow someone to be free or to leave a place
11 take away something or someone and put a new thing there

Word list page 77 **Workbook** page 109

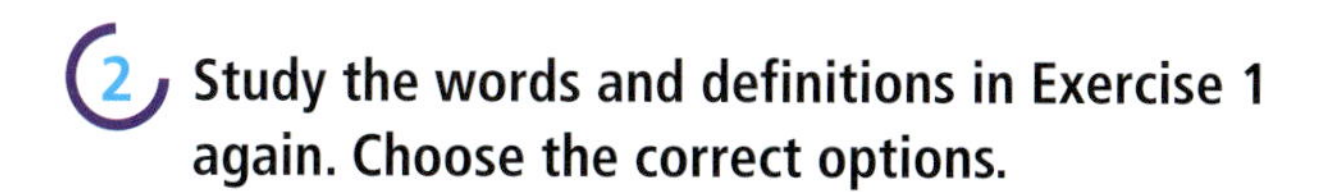

2 **Study the words and definitions in Exercise 1 again. Choose the correct options.**

1 The prefix *dis* / *re* means *again* or *back*.
2 The prefix *dis* / *re* means *not*.

3 **Complete the sentences with words from Exercise 1.**

1 We *researched* the topic of marine archaeology for our history project last week and .... some interesting information.
2 Last week my computer crashed, and all my files .... , but fortunately a computer expert managed to .... most of the information.
3 I don't .... Tanya, but we .... about so many things that we often argue.
4 The old arcades on the pier were .... last month and .... with new 3D machines.
5 My laptop broke down, and I need to .... my files, but the software I have to buy has been .... .
6 A burglar broke into the local pet shop and .... all the animals. The pet shop owner .... them later hiding in the park.

4 **What about you? In pairs, ask and answer.**

1 Has anything ever mysteriously disappeared from your room/bag/desk? What?
2 Do you disagree with your parents/brother/sister/friends about any issues? Which?
3 Would you like to research a particular topic in science/history/geography? Why?/Why not?

Brain Trainer Unit 6 Activity 3
Go to page 116

Chatroom Asking for and giving directions

Speaking and Listening

1 Look at the photo. Does Yasmin want to visit the monument? Does Fraser?

2 Listen and read the conversation. Check your answers.
2.32

3 Listen and read again. Answer the questions.
2.32

1 When was the Pilgrim Monument built?
between 1907 and 1910
2 What can you do at the Pilgrim Monument?
3 What does Fraser want to do?
4 What does Yasmin want to do?
5 What are Fraser and Yasmin looking for?

4 Act out the conversation in groups of four.

Fraser Wow, look at that tower! Does your aunt live here, Yasmin?
Yasmin Don't be silly! This is the Pilgrim Monument.
Fraser When was it built?
Yasmin It was built between 1907 and 1910.
Fraser Are people allowed to visit it?
Yasmin Yes, of course. There is also a pier and a pirate shipwreck museum just a few blocks from here.
Fraser Let's go there now. I've been researching pirates for my history project. This is perfect.
Yasmin Sorry, Fraser. My aunt's expecting us, and we're late and lost. Let's ask for directions.
Fraser Excuse me, how do we get to Standish Street?
Man Go past the monument, and then take the second turn on the left. Is that correct?
Woman No, that's completely wrong! Cross the street in front of the monument. Then turn left and take the first right. You can't miss it.
Yasmin Thanks so much. Sorry to trouble you!

Say it in your language ...
Don't be silly!
Sorry to trouble you!

5 Look back at the conversation. Complete the sentences.

1 Excuse me, *how do we get* to Standish Street?
2 .... the monument.
3 Take the .... on the .... .
4 Cross the street .... .
5 Then .... left, and .... the first right.

6 Read the phrases for asking for and giving directions.

Asking for directions
Excuse me, could you tell me where the post office is?
Excuse me, how do I get to the park?
Excuse me, could you give me directions to the station?

Giving directions
Cross the street next to the bank.
Take the third turn on the left/right.
Turn left/right from here.
Go past the bike store, and then turn left/right.
Take the first left/right.
It's on the left/right.
You can't miss it.

7 Listen to the conversation. Act out the conversation in pairs. 2.33

Holly Excuse me, could you tell me where the movie theater is?
Woman Yes, of course. Turn left at the bookstore and take the first turn on the right. It's across from the coffee shop.
Holly Thank you!

8 Look at the map. Work in pairs. Practice giving directions to these places.

1 supermarket
2 hospital
3 drugstore
4 bookstore
5 park
6 cell phone store

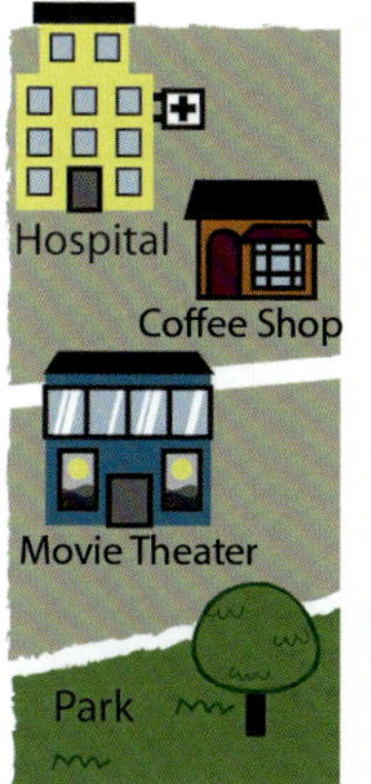

Grammar • Passive questions

Present simple
Are people allowed to visit it?
Where is cocoa produced?
Past simple
When was it built?
Were the buildings restored after the fire?
Future simple
What will be built there in the future?
Will the painting be shown in the art gallery?

Grammar reference Workbook page 96

1 Study the grammar table. Match the beginnings (1–3) to the endings of the sentences (a–c) to complete the rules.

1 Present simple questions are formed with
2 Past simple questions are formed with
3 Future simple questions are formed with

a *was/were* + past participle. The subject comes after *was/were*.
b *am/is/are* + past participle. The subject comes after *am/is/are*.
c *will* + *be* + past participle. The subject comes after *will* and before *be*.

2 Make questions.

1 pier / was / the / When / built?
When was the pier built?
2 it / destroyed / How / was?
3 injured / any / in / fire / the / people / Were?
4 new / designed / Will / pier / be / a?
5 the / Are / of / pier / taken / many / photographs?

3 Listen to the questions and check your answers. Then listen again and take notes on the answers. 2.34

Reading

1 Read the article quickly. Write the dates for these events.

1 Blackbeard captured *La Concorde*. *1717*
2 *Queen Anne's Revenge* sank.
3 Blackbeard was killed.
4 The remains of *Queen Anne's Revenge* were discovered.

Shipwrecks, Pirates and a Sunken Treasure!

Discover the world of Blackbeard

Today marine archaeologist Thelma Broad tells us about Blackbeard's ship!

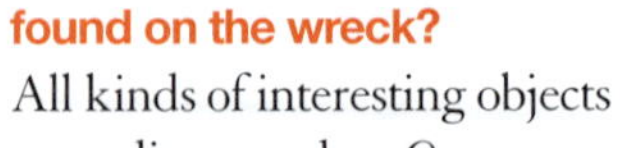

Who was Blackbeard?

Blackbeard was a pirate. His real name was Edward Teach, and he lived from 1680 to 1718. In 1717 he captured a French slave ship called *La Concorde*. He renamed the ship *Queen Anne's Revenge*. This then became his main pirate ship, and he cruised around the the Caribbean, attacking other ships and stealing their treasure.

How did *Queen Anne's Revenge* sink?

In May 1718, Blackbeard sailed *Queen Anne's Revenge* from Charleston, South Carolina, in the US, to North Carolina. Here the ship got stuck in the sea floor and sank. Blackbeard was killed a few months later.

When was the wreck of *Queen Anne's Revenge* discovered?

In 1996 a private research company found the remains of *Queen Anne's Revenge* off the coast of North Carolina.

What kinds of objects were found on the wreck?

All kinds of interesting objects were discovered on *Queen Anne's Revenge*, including plates, guns and jewelry. In total, over 16,000 objects were recovered from the wreck between 1997 and 2012, giving us a glimpse into the daily lives and habits of eighteenth-century pirates.

How are the objects cleaned?

It is a very slow process. They have been underwater for such a long time that there is a thick, hard cover around them. Marine archaeologists X-ray the objects in order to find out what is underneath the cover. Then chemicals are used to remove the cover gently. Most objects are put in a chemical bath for about five years!

Have archaeologists discovered any gold?

Yes! Marine archaeologists have found some gold dust, but they haven't found any coins. Blackbeard and his crew probably removed all the coins and other expensive objects before they abandoned the ship.

Key Words

cruise	stuck	sink
remains	dust	abandon

2 Read the article again. Answer the questions. 2.35

1 What was Blackbeard's real name?
Edward Teach
2 What is the connection between *La Concorde* and *Queen Anne's Revenge*?
3 Where did Blackbeard sail in May 1718?
4 Who found the wreck of *Queen Anne's Revenge* in 1996?
5 How many objects were recovered from the wreck between 1997 and 2012?
6 Why weren't there any expensive objects in the wreck?

Listening

1 Listen to a tour guide talking about the *Cutty Sark*. Choose the best description. 2.36

The *Cutty Sark* was
1 a ship and then a school for sailors.
2 a ship and then a restaurant.
3 a ship and then a home for old sailors.

Listening Bank Unit 6 page 119

2 In pairs, ask and answer.

1 The restoration of the *Cutty Sark* was expensive. Do you think it cost too much?
2 What do you think people can learn about when they visit the *Cutty Sark*?
3 Have you ever visited a historical ship? What was it like?

Writing • A field trip report

1 Read the Writing File.

Writing File Planning a field trip report

When you write a field trip report, divide your information into clear paragraphs or sections.

- **Section 1:** Give a brief summary of the basic information: what you did, why, when and where.
- **Section 2:** Write a description of the trip in clear chronological order.
- **Section 3:** Use the information from your trip to draw conclusions.

2 Look at the sentences. Decide if they come from Section 1, 2 or 3.

Seawall at Goleta Beach

1 In conclusion, we discovered that there are different ways of managing coastal erosion. *3*
2 On Tuesday, October 25, Class 9C traveled to Goleta Beach in California.
3 We looked at the new structures that were built to protect the beach.
4 Our goal was to research coastal erosion and to find out about different ways of managing it.
5 Our first visit in the morning was to Goleta Beach.
6 We also concluded that the use of seawalls in some areas can increase coastal erosion in other areas.

3 Use the phrases in the box to complete this field trip report.

In conclusion	In the afternoon, we	~~Our goal was~~
Our first visit	We also concluded	

On Friday, May 5, Class 10P traveled to Weston-super-Mare. [1] *Our goal was* to research the redevelopment of the Grand Pier and its impact on tourism.

[2] .... was to the Grand Pier. We interviewed the manager of the rebuilt pavilion and found out about the costs of the pier restoration program. [3] .... divided into groups and did surveys of tourists to the town. We asked questions about why they were visiting Weston-super-Mare. We discovered that the main reasons for visiting Weston-super-Mare were the beach, the pier, the arcades and the go-cart track at the pavilion. Some tourists also came for the water sports or to visit relatives.

[4] .... , we discovered that although the reconstruction of the pier was very expensive, it was also an important tourist attraction for the town. [5] .... that the town could attract more tourists by improving its water sports facilities.

4 You are going to write a short field trip report about a visit to an interesting tourist attraction in your country.

Think about
- when it was built
- how many people visit it
- if it was ever damaged or restored

Complete these notes.
Field trip to: ....
Aim: Find out about ....
Conclusion: Is .... a good tourist attraction?

5 Now write your report. Use the sample field trip report in Exercise 3 and your notes in Exercise 4.

Remember!
- Plan your report carefully and divide it into sections.
- Use the vocabulary in this unit.
- Check your grammar, spelling and punctuation.

Refresh Your Memory!

Grammar • Review

1 Are the sentences active (A) or passive (P)?

1 The Bell Rock Lighthouse was built in 1811. *P*
2 It was designed by Robert Stevenson and John Rennie.
3 They started working on the lighthouse in 1807.
4 It was built of white stone.
5 Stevenson wrote a book about it.
6 People call it Stevenson's Lighthouse.
7 It is still used as a working lighthouse today.

2 Make these sentences passive.

1 A builder restored my house.
My house *was restored by a builder.*
2 They sell delicious food at this store.
Delicious food .... .
3 We don't keep the bread in this cabinet.
The bread .... .
4 They will take the photograph this afternoon.
The photograph .... .
5 Someone stole my bag yesterday.
My bag .... .
6 A lot of tourists visit this attraction.
This attraction .... .
7 They won't fix my car this week.
My car .... .
8 They sent the postcard yesterday.
The postcard .... .

3 Make questions. Then match the questions (1–5) to the answers (a–e).

1 was / *Treasure Island* / When / the / written / book
When was the book Treasure Island *written?*
2 by / was / written / Who / it
3 a / Was / book / made / into / movie / the
4 lot / Is / today / read / people / it / by / of / a
5 book / sold / is / the / Where

a Yes. It is still read by many people today.
b Robert Louis Stevenson
c In 1883. *1*
d In all good bookstores.
e Yes. The book was made into several movies.

Vocabulary • Review

4 Match (1–5) to (a–e) to make words about coastal life.

1 hot	a gull
2 beach	b shop
3 souvenir	c chair
4 go-	d dog stand
5 sea	e carts

5 Complete the sentences with the correct form of the verbs.

~~discontinue~~	discover	dislike	recover
remove	replace	research	restore

1 You can't buy this cell phone in the stores—it was *discontinued* last year.
2 Could you .... your bag from the chair? I want to sit down.
3 I was sick over the weekend, but I've .... .
4 I want to .... my old bike with a new one.
5 I don't .... Leo, but we're not best friends.
6 Look! I .... $10 in my pocket!
7 My family moved into an old lighthouse last year and .... it.
8 I'm .... my family history at the moment.

Speaking • Review

6 Complete the conversation with these phrases. Then listen and check. 2.37

~~Could you tell me~~	cross the street	Go past
how do I get to	Turn right	You can't miss it!

A Excuse me. [1] *Could you tell me* where the station is?
B Yes, of course. It's across from the library. [2] ....
A Ah, but [3] .... the library?
B OK. [4] .... from here, and then [5] .... next to the bookstore. [6] .... the school, and then turn left.

Dictation

7 Listen and write in your notebook. 2.38

My assessment profile: Workbook page 132

Reading

1 Read Laura's profile. Look at the photos and the headline. Guess what Laura has achieved.

a She has written a book about sailing.
b She has designed and made her own boat.
c She has sailed around the world.
d She has built a house shaped like a boat.

2 Read the article. Answer the questions.

2.39

1 How old was Laura when her family moved to the Netherlands?
She was four years old.
2 Where did Laura sail on her first solo journey?
3 Why did some people disagree with Laura's plans to sail around the world alone?
4 What was Laura doing when she was found in St. Maarten?
5 How old was Laura when she completed her solo around-the-world trip?
6 What did she eat when she was sailing around the world?

Born to Sail

Laura Dekker was born on a boat and lived there with her parents for the first four years of her life as they completed a seven-year trip around the world. When that journey ended in 1999, Laura's family settled in the Netherlands, but her love of sailing and the ocean grew stronger every day.

When she was six years old, she was given her own boat and learned to sail it. She soon began to make short solo sailing trips. At the age of thirteen, Laura made her first long solo journey from the Netherlands to Britain. Laura then started to plan a journey around the world, but although many people admired her courage and determination, other people disagreed and felt that she was too young to sail alone. The Dutch authorities tried to stop her. "The journey is too dangerous for a thirteen-year-old, and her education will be disturbed," they said. A few months later, Laura ran away from home and was discovered in St. Maarten in the Caribbean. She was trying to buy a boat!

Finally, in July 2010, when Laura was fourteen years old, the Dutch authorities removed the ban on her record-breaking attempt. She began her journey in August 2011, and on January 21, 2012, at sixteen years and four months old, she arrived in St. Maarten and became the youngest person to sail solo around the world.

During her journey, she had to deal with six-meter-high waves, storms and strong winds. She lived on a diet of pasta, rice, crackers and pancakes. She kept her boat and herself safe from bad weather and also from pirates, and she even did some homework as well!

Class discussion

1 What do you think? Was Laura too young to sail solo around the world?
2 How do you think Laura felt during her journey? Why?
3 Would you like to do what Laura did? Why?/Why not?
4 What would you miss most if you sailed around the world?

Grammar • Modals: ability, obligation, prohibition, advice

1 Complete the second sentence so that it means the same as the first. Use the verbs given. There may be more than one possible answer.

1 It's not necessary to wear a helmet when you ride a scooter.
You *don't have to wear a helmet* when you ride a scooter.
2 I advise you to take some food to the party.
You .... to the party.
3 It's a bad idea to forget your sister's birthday.
You .... sister's birthday.
4 Leave your bags outside the classroom!
You .... outside the classroom.
5 No talking in the library!
We .... in the library.
6 She is able to play the guitar, but she isn't able to play the piano.
She .... the guitar, but she .... the piano.

• Past modals

2 Put these sentences into the past tense.

1 Sarah can't read well without her glasses.
Sarah couldn't read well without her glasses.
2 We have to take the dog for a walk.
3 They don't have to study over summer break.
4 I can hear you, but I can't see you.
5 They must be at the theater at 6 o'clock.

• Modals: possibility

3 Choose the correct options.

A Is this John's bag?
B No, it [1] *can't* / *could* be John's bag. John's bag is blue, and this one is red.
A Well, it [2] *must* / *could* be Henry's bag. His is red.
B Yes, it [3] *could* / *can't* be Henry's, or it [4] *might* / *must* be Jade's. Her bag is red, too.
A Let's look inside. Aha, this book has Jade's name in it.
B So it [5] *must* / *can't* be Jade's bag!

• Will/Going to

4 Choose the correct options.

1 **A** I'm hungry.
B I'*m going to* / *'ll* make you a sandwich.
2 **A** What *are you going to* / *will you* do over the summer break?
B We*'re going to* / *will* sail the ocean!
3 Oh no! It's 8 o'clock already. We*'re going to* / *will* miss the bus.
4 **A** Where do you think you *are going to* / *will* live in 2020?
B I think I*'m going to* / *'ll* live on my own private island!
5 **A** *Are you going to* / *Will you* go to Amy's birthday party tonight?
B Yes, I *am* / *will*. How about you?
A No, I can't. But I've already sent her a card.

5 Complete the sentences with *will* or *going to* and the verbs in parentheses.

1 I think my team *will win* (win) the next game.
2 My friends and I .... (meet) at the movie theater tomorrow at 5 o'clock, but I don't know which movie we .... (see) yet.
3 **A** Oh no! The car's not working.
B Don't worry. We .... (take) the bus to school.
4 I broke my brother's new cell phone.
He .... (be) really angry with me!
5 What .... (study) in college next year?

• Present simple and Present continuous for future

6 Complete the text with the Present simple or Present continuous form of the verbs in parentheses.

I'm looking forward to tomorrow—I have a lot of plans. My singing lesson [1] *starts* (start) at 9 a.m., and it [2] .... (end) at 10:30 a.m. Then I [3] .... (meet) my friends in the park. In the afternoon, we [4] .... (take) a train to Philadelphia. The train [5] .... (leave) at 3:30 p.m. We [6] .... (visit) the Rodin Museum, and then we [7] .... (go) to the theater in the evening. What [8] .... (you/do) tomorrow?

• Passive statements

7 Make these sentences passive.

1 People make chocolate from cacao beans.
Chocolate *is made from cacao beans.*
2 They produce Sony computers in Japan.
Sony computers .... .
3 They won't clean your windows tomorrow.
Your windows .... .
4 Someone broke this plate yesterday.
This plate .... .
5 Van Gogh didn't paint the *Mona Lisa*.
The *Mona Lisa* .... .
6 People will discover new sources of energy in the future.
New sources of energy .... .

8 Complete the text with the correct passive form of the verbs in parentheses.

In the past, most clothes [1] *were made* (make) out of natural materials like leather or cotton, and they [2] .... (sew) by hand at home. Now man-made materials like polyester [3] .... (use), and most clothes [4] .... (make) in factories. Who knows how our clothes [5] .... (produce) in the future? Perhaps new materials [6] .... (discover).

• Passive questions

9 Make these questions passive.

1 Who makes this beautiful jewelry?
Who is this beautiful jewelry made by?
2 When did they set up the company?
3 Does your teacher check your homework?
4 Will they decorate your room on Tuesday?
5 How did they find the shipwreck?

10 Make passive questions for these answers. Use the question words.

1 My bag is made of leather and metal. (What)
What is your bag made of?
2 This house was built in 1910. (When)
3 The book will be published by Penguin Books. (Who)
4 The poem was written by Pablo Neruda. (Who)
5 These flowers are grown in Holland. (Where)

Speaking • Asking for clarification

1 Put the conversation in the correct order.

☐ a Oh, I see! Thanks.
☐ b Yes, I know. But all the streets are closed to traffic today.
[1] c We can't take the bus to the community center today.
☐ d No, the bike race is on the streets! But we can walk to the community center.
☐ e What do you mean? We always go by bus.
☐ f It's because of the bike race.
☐ g Are you saying that there's a bike race at the community center?
☐ h Sorry, I don't understand. Why are the streets closed?

• Phone language

2 Choose the correct options to complete the conversation.

A Hello, Redhill Bookstore, can I help you?
B Hello, [1] *I'd like* / *I like* to speak to the manager, please.
A I'm sorry, he's talking to a customer at the moment. [2] *Can* / *Do* I take a message?
B Yes, please. My name's Emma Moore. I'm calling [3] *after* / *about* the salesperson job.
A Oh, the manager's free now. [4] *Hold* / *Wait* on, please. I'll [5] *transfer* / *put* you to him now.

• Asking for and giving directions

3 Complete the conversations with these phrases.

can't miss	Cross	~~give me directions~~
Go past	how do I	on the right
the second turn	turn left	

A Excuse me, could you [1] *give me directions* to the library?
B Yes, of course. [2] .... the street next to the school. Then take [3] .... on the right. It's [4] .... .
A Thank you so much.

A Excuse me, [5] .... get to the park?
B [6] .... the bank, and then [7] .... . You [8] .... it.
A Thank you.

Review 2

Vocabulary • Natural disasters

1 Complete the words for natural disasters.

1 ts*unam*i
2 f_m_ _e
3 dr_ _ _ht
4 e_ _t_qu_ _e
5 fl_ _d
6 a_a_ _ _ch_
7 h_r_ _ _ _ _e
8 di_ea_ _

• Phrasal verbs 2

2 Complete the sentences with these words.

across	down (x2)	forward to
~~off~~	~~on~~	on
out (x2)	through	

1 It was very hot, so I took *off* my sweater and put *on* some sunscreen.
2 If your car breaks .... on the highway or runs .... of gas, you should call for roadside assistance.
3 If you stop panicking and calm .... , we will be able to get .... this situation without an accident.
4 I came .... an interesting article in the newspaper a few days ago.
5 Are you looking .... your vacation next week?
6 Let's keep .... trying to fix this engine—I'm sure we can figure .... what's wrong with it.

• Work collocations

3 Choose the correct options.

1 *answer* / *prepare* the phone
2 *make* / *take* an appointment
3 *check* / *work* at the front desk
4 *deal* / *make* some copies
5 *prepare* / *give* a spreadsheet
6 *attend* / *write* a report
7 *deal* / *attend* a meeting
8 *order* / *give* a presentation
9 *check* / *attend* emails
10 *take* / *answer* payments
11 *give* / *order* office supplies
12 *give* / *deal* with inquiries

• Job qualities

4 Read the sentences (1–4) and then match two descriptions from the box to each name.

excellent IT skills	experienced	good communicator
~~patient~~	practical	punctual
~~reliable~~	team player	

Jim: *patient, reliable* **Dan:** .... , ...
Helen: .... , ... **Kerry:** .... , ...

1 Jim doesn't get angry easily, and you can always trust him.
2 Helen is never late, and she can do useful things.
3 Dan is good at using a computer, and he likes working with other people.
4 Kerry has had this job for ten years, and she is good at talking to people.

• Coastal life

5 Complete the words.

1 You can buy presents for your friends in a s*ouveni*r shop.
2 A common coastal bird is a s_ _g _ll.
3 You can sit in a b _ _ _ h c _ _ _ r on the beach.
4 If you're hungry, you can buy a h_t d_ _ and then go to an i_e cr_ _m s_ _nd.
5 There is often an ar_ _d_ near the pi_ _.
6 Get some shade under a b_ _ ch u_ _ _ _ _ la.

• Verbs with prefixes *dis-* and *re-*

6 Match the verbs (a–h) to the definitions (1–8).

1 think someone is wrong *b*
2 allow someone to leave a place
3 find something
4 take something away from somewhere
5 find out information about something
6 not like someone/something
7 get better
8 stop making something

a research
b disagree
c dislike
d remove
e release
f discover
g recover
h discontinue

Word list

Unit 4 • Survive!

Natural disasters

avalanche	/ˈævəˌlæntʃ/
bury	/ˈbɛri/
destroy	/dɪˈstrɔɪ/
disease	/dɪˈziz/
drought	/draʊt/
drown	/draʊn/
earthquake	/ˈɚθkweɪk/
erupt	/ɪˌrʌpt/
famine	/ˈfæmɪn/
flood	/flʌd/
hurricane	/ˈhɚɪˌkeɪn, ˈhʌr-/
spread	/sprɛd/
starve	/stɑrv/
survive	/sɚˈvaɪv/
tsunami	/tsʊˈnɑmi/
volcano	/vɑlˈkeɪnoʊ/

Phrasal verbs 2

break down	/ˌbreɪk ˈdaʊn/
calm down	/ˌkɑm ˈdaʊn/
come across	/ˌkʌm əˈkrɔs/
figure out	/ˌfɪgyɚ ˈaʊt/
get through	/ˌgɛt ˈθru/
keep on	/ˌkip ˈɔn/
look forward to	/ˌlʊk ˈfɔrwɚd tə/
put on	/ˈpʊt ˈɔn/
run out of	/ˌrʌn ˈaʊt əv/
take off	/ˌteɪk ˈɔf/

Unit 5 • Work for It

Work collocations

answer the phone	/ˈænsɚ ðə ˈfoʊn/
attend a meeting	/əˌtɛnd ə ˈmiṭ ɪŋ/
check emails	/ˌtʃɛk ˈimeɪlz/
deal with inquiries	/ˌdil wɪð ɪnˈkwaɪəriz/
give a presentation	/ˌgɪv ə prɛzənˈteɪʃən/
make an appointment	/ˌmeɪk ən əˈpɔɪntˈmənt/
make some copies	/ˌmeɪk səm ˈkɑpiz/
order office supplies	/ˌɔrdɚ ˈɔfɪs səˌplaɪz/
prepare a spreadsheet	/prɪˌpɛr ə ˈsprɛdʃit/
take payments	/ˌteɪk ˈpeɪmənts/
work at the front desk	/ˈwɚk ət ðə ˌfrʌnt ˈdɛsk/
write a report	/ˌraɪt ə rɪˈpɔrt/

Job qualities

accurate	/ˈækyərɪt/
analytical	/ˌænlˈɪṭ ɪkəl/
excellent IT skills	/ˈɛksələnt ˌaɪ ˈti ˌskɪlz/
experienced	/ɪkˈspɪriənst/
good communicator	/ˌgʊd kəˈmyunəˌkeɪtɚ/
leadership qualities	/ˈlidɚˌʃɪp ˈkwɑləṭ iz/
organized	/ˈɔrgəˌnaɪzd/
patient	/ˈpeɪʃənt/
practical	/ˈpræktɪkəl/
punctual	/ˈpʌŋktʃuəl/
reliable	/rɪˈlaɪəbəl/
team player	/ˈtim ˌpleɪɚ/

Unit 6 • Coast

Coastal life

arcade	/ɑrˈkeɪd/
beach chair	/ˈbitʃ tʃɛr/
beach umbrella	/ˈbitʃ ʌmˈbrɛlə/
cliffs	/klɪfs/
go-cart	/ˈgoʊkɑrt/
harbor	/ˈhɑrbɚ/
hot dog stand	/ˈhɑt dɔg ˈstænd/
ice cream stand	/ˈaɪs krim ˈstænd/
pier	/pɪr/
seagull	/ˈsigʌl/
seawall	/ˈsiwɔl/
souvenir shop	/ˌsuvəˈnɪr ˈʃɑp/

Verbs with prefixes *dis-* and *re-*

disagree	/ˌdɪsəˈgri/
disappear	/ˌdɪsəˈpɪr/
discontinue	/ˌdɪskənˈtɪnyu/
discover	/dɪˈskʌvɚ/
dislike	/dɪsˈlaɪk/
recover	/rɪˈkʌvɚ/
release	/rɪˈlis/
remove	/rɪˈmuv/
replace	/rɪˈpleɪs/
research	/ˈrisɚtʃ, rɪˈsɚtʃ/
restore	/rɪˈstɔr/

Final Frontiers

Grammar
First and Second conditional; Subject/Object questions

Vocabulary
Adjective antonyms; Space

Speaking
Giving warnings

Writing
An application letter

Word list page 111
Workbook page 110

Vocabulary • Adjective antonyms

1 3.1 **Match the words in the first box to the opposite words in the second box. Some words can make two pairs. Then listen, check and repeat.**

ancient *modern*	deep	light	low
narrow	ordinary	permanent	weak

dark	heavy
high	~~modern~~
powerful	shallow
strange	strong
temporary	wide

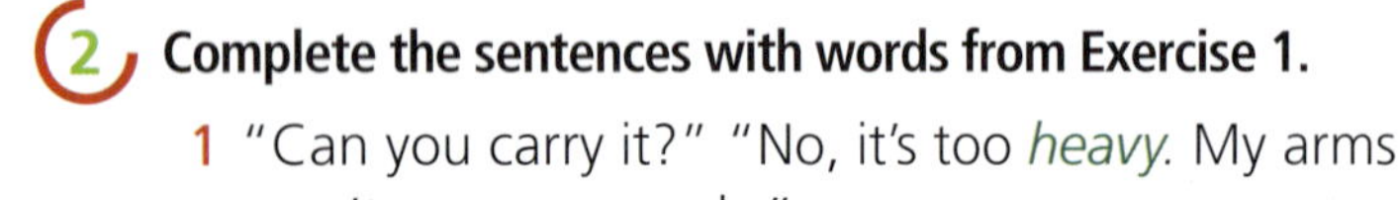

2 Complete the sentences with words from Exercise 1.

1 "Can you carry it?" "No, it's too *heavy*. My arms aren't *strong* enough."
2 The plane has a very .... engine, so it can go really fast and really .... up in the sky.
3 Green Street is our .... address. We're moving to our .... home next month.
4 I love the new, ... buildings in Beijing and also the .... ones that were built 600 years ago.
5 The river is .... here. Over there it's too .... to cross.
6 The baby bird is very .... . We think it might die.
7 "Why is he wearing purple pants? He looks really .... ." "He isn't wearing his .... clothes because he's doing a comedy show today."
8 The water in the lake is .... . Children play in it, but you can't swim because it isn't .... enough.
9 In summer, it's still .... at ten o'clock at night, because the sun goes down very late. But in winter, it gets .... at four in the afternoon.
10 The wall's .... , so it's safe to jump over it.

3 In pairs, describe the photos. Use adjectives from Exercise 1.

The cave in photo 4 is dark, deep and narrow.

3.2, 3.3 **Pronunciation Unit 7** page 121

Brain Trainer Unit 7 Activities 1 and 2
Go to page 116

Reading

1 **Look at the photos. What can you see in them?**

2 **Read the article quickly. Match the headings (1–3) to the paragraphs (A–C).**

1 A world of water
2 New plants, new people
3 Underground secrets

Explorers: Where Next?

The explorers of the past were the first to see new continents, reach the poles or sail around the world. But what on earth can the people of tomorrow discover?

A ....

The biggest rain forest in southern Africa was discovered in Mozambique only a few years ago, with the help of Google Earth™. Perhaps there are other unknown rain forests waiting for discovery. There are probably about thirty thousand species of rain forest plants and animals that we know nothing about. There are also rain forest tribes that have had no contact with the modern world.

If we were friends with these tribes, we would probably know a lot more about medicinal plants. There's definitely more to discover in the rain forests.

B ....

In the US alone, people find about 1,000 new caves every year. In fact, we know more about Mars than about the underground places on Earth! You'd soon discover something exciting if you spent a lot of time spelunking: a strange new animal species, or some beautiful crystal flowers, or even an ancient painting.

C ....

You'll have a good chance of discovering something new if you look in the oceans. There are ancient cities which have disappeared underwater after earthquakes and floods. There are canyons six times deeper than the Grand Canyon and more active volcanoes beneath the sea than above it. If you want to see something down there, you'll need a strong light, because below 200 meters, it's completely dark. But we have only explored about five percent of the earth's oceans. There's a lot more to find!

3 3.4 **Read the article again. Answer the questions.**

1 How did people discover a new rain forest?
With the help of Google Earth ™.
2 Why does the text mention the number 30,000?
3 Why is it useful to make contact with rain forest tribes?
4 What might you find in a cave? List three things.
5 Why are there underwater cities?
6 What is useful when you are exploring underwater? Why?

4 **What about you? Ask and answer in pairs.**

1 Would you like to explore these places? Why?/Why not?
2 Where else can we explore?
3 Do you think it's better to be an explorer today or an explorer in the past? Why?

Grammar • First and Second conditional

First conditional
If you want to see something, you'll need a strong light.

Second conditional
If we were friends with these tribes, we would know a lot more.

Grammar reference Workbook page 98

1 **Study the grammar table. Copy and complete the table with these words.**

impossible past possible ~~present~~ will would

	First conditional	Second conditional
if clause	1 *Present* simple	2 .... simple
main clause	3	4 ....
use	5 .... situations in the future	unlikely or 6 .... situations in the present or future

2 **Choose the correct options.**

1 If you *explore* / *will explore* the oceans, you'll find some amazing fish.
2 The camera will take photos of the ocean floor if it *doesn't break* / *won't break* in the deep water.
3 He *is* / *will be* happy if he finds a new species.
4 If we *dive* / *will dive* below 200 meters, the water will be completely dark.
5 We *don't see* / *won't see* anything if we don't bring flashlights.
6 If you scream, people *hear* / *will hear* you.

3 **Complete the sentences with the correct form of the verbs.**

1 If I were a climber, I *would want* (want) to climb Machapuchare ("Fish Tail Mountain") in Nepal.
2 However, I would get into trouble if the Nepalese .... (find) me there.
3 According to their beliefs, the god Shiva .... (not like) it if someone climbed up to his sacred home.
4 If the Nepalese .... (not have) these beliefs, people would try to climb Machapuchare.
5 If anyone reached the top, they .... (see) a view that no one has ever seen before.

4 **Complete the email with the correct form of the verbs. Use the First or Second conditional.**

New Message

Hi Lily,

I'm in Antarctica! I'd be cold if I [1] *didn't have* (not have) the right equipment, but I'm OK in my warm coat. If you [2] .... (be) here, you'd love it!

We [3] .... (start) our journey to the ice caves tomorrow if there isn't too much wind. If we [4] .... (reach) the caves, I'll take a lot of photos.

I [5] .... (prefer) it if I had my big camera with me, but if I packed it in my bag, there [6] .... (not be) any space for my clothes! I hope my little camera will work OK. If we [7] .... (be) lucky with the weather, we'll stay at the caves for two weeks. The Internet [8] .... (not work) there if the weather is bad, but I'll send another email as soon as I can.

Love,
Adam

5 **Complete the sentences so they are true for you.**

1 I'd be really scared if …
2 My parents would worry if …
3 My friends will be really happy if …
4 If I arrived at school an hour late, …

6 **Complete the questions with the correct form of these verbs.**

ask can choose ~~do~~ give

1 If it's sunny this weekend, what *will you do* (you)?
2 If you .... go to any country in the world, where would you go?
3 If you had to learn a new sport, which sport .... (you)?
4 If someone .... you some money for your birthday, what will you spend it on?
5 If you were in trouble, who .... (you) for help?

7 **Work in pairs. Ask and answer the questions in Exercise 6.**

If it's sunny this weekend, I'll probably go to the beach.

Vocabulary • Space

1 3.5 **Match these words to the items in the picture (1–12). Then listen, check and repeat.**

asteroid	astronaut	astronomer	comet *1*
galaxy	moon	orbit	planet
solar system	spacecraft	~~star~~	telescope

Word list page 111 **Workbook** page 110

2 Complete the sentences with words from Exercise 1.

1 I can see thousands of *stars* in the sky tonight.
2 A .... is a large group of stars.
3 Mars is a .... in our solar system.
4 An .... is smaller than a planet. Sometimes these objects crash into Earth.
5 Earth is one of the eight planets in our .... .
6 You will need a .... to see the planets clearly.
7 An .... is a person who studies space.
8 In the night sky, a .... looks like a star with a tail.
9 An .... is a person who travels into space.
10 A planet's .... is its path around the sun.
11 The .... creates the biggest light in the sky at night.
12 Astronauts travel through space in a .... .

Brain Trainer Unit 7 Activity 3
Go to page 116

3 Take the quiz. Then check your answers in the box below.

SPACE QUIZ

TEST YOUR SPACE KNOWLEDGE!

TRUE (T) OR FALSE (F)?

1 Earth's orbit around the sun takes one month. *F*
2 Venus is the biggest planet in our solar system.
3 There are billions of galaxies, and each galaxy has at least ten million stars.
4 A star is a sun in a different solar system from our own.
5 The first astronaut went to Mars in 1989.
6 The most powerful telescope on Earth is in the desert in Chile.
7 The planet Jupiter has 67 moons.
8 There are rings around the planet Neptune.
9 We last saw Halley's Comet without a telescope in 1986, and we will see it next in 2061.

1 F (It takes one year.) **2** F (Jupiter) **3** T **4** T
5 F (No astronauts have been to Mars.) **6** T **7** T
8 T **9** T

Chatroom Giving warnings

Speaking and Listening

1 Look at the photo. Answer the questions.

1 What did Fraser get for his birthday?
2 What can Yasmin see?
3 Why are Archie and Fraser laughing?

2 Listen and read the conversation. Check your answers. 3.6

3 Listen and read again. Answer the questions. 3.6

1 Where did the telescope come from?
It was Fraser's birthday present from his uncle.
2 What is Fraser's uncle's job?
3 What might make you blind?
4 Is it daytime or nighttime?
5 What does Yasmin think she can see in the telescope?
6 What can she really see?

4 Act out the conversation in groups of three.

Yasmin What did you get for your birthday, Fraser?
Fraser Come and see.
Archie Wow! A telescope! Who gave it to you?
Fraser My uncle. He's an astronomer.
Archie Cool job! What does he study?
Fraser Comets, I think.
Archie Can I look through the telescope?
Fraser OK, but make sure you don't break it. And be careful not to look at the sun with it.
Archie Why? What happens?
Fraser It damages your eyes. You might even go blind.
Yasmin Chill out, Fraser! That shouldn't be a problem now. It's dark outside. Can I take a look?
Fraser Sure. But I wouldn't press the red button if I were you. It changes the direction of the …
Yasmin Wow! I can see an orange planet really clearly. This is incredible!
Fraser Yasmin! That's my lamp!
Yasmin Oh! Uh … I knew that!

Say it in your language …
Chill out!
This is incredible!

5 **Look back at the conversation. Complete these sentences.**

1 *Make sure* you don't break it.
2 .... not to look at the sun with it.
3 I wouldn't press the red button if I ....

6 **Read the phrases for giving warnings.**

Giving warnings
Make sure you don't ...
Watch out for the ...
Be careful not to ...
I wouldn't ... if I were you.

7 3.7 **Listen to the conversations. What dangers do the speakers mention? Act out the conversations in pairs.**

Fraser I'm going to [1] take my telescope to the park.
Yasmin OK, but I wouldn't [2] go there alone at night if I were you. It's dangerous. And make sure you don't [3] forget your flashlight.

Holly I'm going to [4] learn to scuba dive.
Archie That sounds like fun, but watch out for [5] sharks! And be careful not to [6] stay underwater too long.

8 **Work in pairs. Replace the words in purple in Exercise 7. Use these words and/or your own ideas. Act out the conversations.**

I'm going to sail across the Atlantic.

OK, but I wouldn't ...

1 sail across the Atlantic / work for NASA / go to the North Pole
2 do it on your own / become an astronaut / go there in winter
3 fall out of the boat / crash any spacecraft / forget your gloves
4 climb a mountain / go spelunking / go on a space flight
5 avalanches / scary bats / aliens
6 fall off a cliff / get lost underground / open the window

Grammar • Subject/Object questions

Subject questions
What happens if I press this button?
Who gave it to you?
Object questions
What does he do all day?
What did you get for your birthday?

Grammar reference Workbook page 98

1 **Study the grammar table. Complete the rules with *subject* or *object*.**

1 When the question word is the .... of the sentence, we make questions with: question word + *do/does/did* + subject + infinitive without *to*.
2 When the question word is the .... of the sentence, we make questions with: question word + Present/Past/Future form of the verb. We don't use *do/does/did*.

2 **Are these object questions (O) or subject questions (S)? Complete the questions.**

1 What *do you want* (you/want) to watch? *O*
2 How many people .... (study) English at your school?
3 What .... (that word/mean)?
4 Who .... (go) to the astronomy club on Fridays?
5 Who .... (drive) you to school in the morning?
6 Who .... (we/know) in Washington, DC?

3 **Make questions. Match them to these answers.**

a kangaroo	~~Canada~~	chocolate
Marco Polo	Roald Amundsen	the US

1 Which country / Leif Eriksson / discover / in the 11th century? *Canada*
2 Who / travel / in China / in the 13th century?
3 What / Hernan Cortes / bring / to Europe / in 1528?
4 What / come / to Europe / on the ship of James Cook / in 1770?
5 Which country / Lewis and Clark / explore / at the beginning of the 19th century?
6 Who / reach / the South Pole / first?

Reading

1 Look at the picture and answer the questions.

If humans started a colony on Mars,

1 would it be easy to spend time outside?
2 how would they build things?
3 where would they live?
4 how would they grow food?

NEXT STOP: MARS

No astronauts have walked on the moon since 1972, but some people think that the days of humans on other planets are not far away. In twenty years, there might even be a permanent colony on Mars.

We asked astronomer Matthew Simmons to tell us more.

What makes Mars a good place for a colony in space?
Of all the planets in our solar system, Mars is the most suitable for human life. A day on Mars is a similar length to our own: 24 hours and 40 minutes. If you lived on Venus, a day would last 243 Earth days! Mars also has seasons like those on Earth. There is ice on Mars too, so if there were colonists there, they would be able to make water.

What problems would the colonists have?
One big problem would be the cold. Mars has an average temperature of -63°C. There's also weaker gravity than on Earth, more radiation from the sun and much less oxygen.

So how would people survive?
Robots would build underground homes before the colonists arrived. There would be big greenhouses too, and these would have a temperature warm enough to grow plants. Perhaps we could send spacecraft full of greenhouse gases to Mars, and over time, change the temperature and atmosphere of the whole planet so it was more like Earth.

How long does the journey to Mars take?
About nine months. But if you went, you'd probably have to stay on Mars for the rest of your life.

No one would volunteer to be a colonist if they could never come home again!
Interestingly, that's not true. When a space magazine wrote about a future colony on Mars, it got letters from more than 400 people who wanted to be part of it.

Key Words

colony/colonist	gravity
radiation	oxygen
greenhouse	atmosphere

2 Read the article quickly and check your answers to Exercise 1.

3 Read the article again. Answer the questions. 3.8

1 Where in space might humans live in the near future? *They might live on Mars.*
2 What is there on Mars that makes it more suitable for human life than other planets?
3 Unfortunately, Mars has a lot more of this than Earth. What is it?
4 How might Mars change in the future?
5 How long would colonists stay on Mars?
6 If there were a colony on Mars, would anyone volunteer to go to it?

4 Find these numbers in the article. Explain what they refer to.

~~1972~~	20	243	-63	9	400

The last person on the moon was there in 1972.

Listening

1 You are going to listen to some ideas of other places where people might build colonies in the future. What places might the speakers mention?

2 Listen to speakers A, B and C. Which types of colonies do they talk about? 3.9

A ....
B ....
C ....

Listening Bank Unit 7 page 120

3 What about you? In pairs, ask and answer the questions.

1 Would you like to be a colonist on Mars or in any of the places in Exercise 2? Why?/Why not?
2 What kind of person would be a good colonist in each of these places?

Writing • An application letter

1 Read the Writing File.

Writing File Letter writing

- If you don't know the name of the person who you are writing to, start with *Dear Sir/Madam.*
- Write the subject of the letter as a heading.
- Give the reason for writing: *I was very interested to see …, I am writing to …*
- In the last paragraph, say what you want to happen next: *I very much hope that you …, I look forward to hearing from you.*
- End with *Sincerely, Yours truly,* or *Regards,* and your name.

2 Read the job ad and application letter. Find language from the Writing File.

Colonists needed

New Frontiers is looking for people to start two exciting new colonies, one on the ocean floor and the other on Mars.

Dear Sir/Madam,

Underwater colony

I was very interested to see your ad. I am writing to apply for a job as an underwater colonist. I have always loved the water, and for many years it has been my dream to find out more about life in the ocean. There are more people and less wildlife in my local area every year. If I lived in an underwater colony, I would be closer to nature, and I would love that.

If I lived in the colony, I would be a useful member of the team. I am a hardworking and flexible person, and I am a good communicator. My favorite hobby is scuba diving, so I already have a lot of experience being underwater. I have never dived in dark water, but I learn new skills quickly.

I very much hope that you will choose me as a colonist. I look forward to hearing from you.

Yours truly,

Jasmine Wilkins

Jasmine Wilkins

3 Read the letter again. Answer the questions.

1 Which colony is Jasmine applying for?
the underwater colony
2 What is her dream?
3 What would she like about living in the colony?
4 What kind of person is she?
5 What useful experience does she have?

4 Fill in the blanks in the reply to Jasmine's letter.

Underwater colony

[1] *Dear* Jasmine,

I was [2] …. to read your application letter. I would like to invite you to an interview at our office at 2 p.m. on Thursday, May 5.

I [3] …. much [4] …. that you can come to the interview.
I look [5] …. to [6] …. from you.

Yours [7] …. ,

Michael de Souza

5 Look back at the article on page 84. Which things would be useful if you lived in a colony on Mars?

1 I go horseback riding every weekend. ✗
2 I have done a lot of spelunking.
3 I have often helped on my family's farm.
4 I have excellent IT skills.
5 I'm practical and reliable.

6 You are going to write a letter applying to be a Mars colonist. Take notes about yourself. Use the questions in Exercise 3 to help you.

7 Write your letter. Use the outline below and your notes from Exercise 6.

1 Opening *Dear Sir/Madam,*
2 Give the reason for writing.
3 Say why the job interests you.
4 Describe your skills, personality and experience.
5 Say what you want to happen next.
6 Closing *Regards*

Remember!

- Only include skills, personality qualities and experiences that might be useful for the job.
- Use phrases from the Writing File.
- Use vocabulary and grammar from this unit.
- Check your grammar, spelling and punctuation.

Refresh Your Memory!

Grammar • Review

1 Are the sentences First conditional (1) or Second conditional (2)? Complete them with the correct form of the verbs.

1 If astronauts went to Venus, they *wouldn't survive* (not survive) the 465°C temperatures. *2*
2 We .... (be) out almost all day if we visit the space museum.
3 If we .... (find) intelligent life on other planets, will it be good or bad news for humans?
4 I'd look at the stars every night if I .... (have) a telescope.
5 What .... (you/do) if you met an alien?
6 She .... (not get) a job at NASA if she doesn't do well on her science exams.

2 Make answers. Use the First or Second conditional.

1 Should I tell Mel? (no / she / tell / everyone)
No. If you tell Mel, she'll tell everyone.
2 Are you getting a job? (yes / I / have / more money)
3 Is he from Chile? (no / he / speak / Spanish)
4 Can we go to Egypt? (probably / we / see / some amazing ancient buildings)
5 Do you like meat? (no / I / not be / a vegetarian)

3 Complete the questions in the conversation. Use the correct form of the verbs in bold.

Harry Lucy **learned** to scuba dive last week.
Grandma Who [1] *learned* to scuba dive?
Harry Lucy. She **had** a nice instructor for her course.
Grandma Who [2] .... for her course?
Harry A nice instructor. But on her first dive, she **broke** her arm on the side of the boat.
Grandma What [3] .... ?
Harry Her arm.
Grandma Oh no! Is she OK?
Harry Yes. Her diving instructor **helped** her.
Grandma Who [4] .... her?
Harry Her instructor. And he **sent** flowers to Lucy every day after that!
Grandma What [5] ....?
Harry Flowers. She **got** flowers from him.
Grandma Who [6] .... flowers?
Harry Lucy!

Vocabulary • Review

4 Complete the sentences with these words.

heavy	low	modern	narrow
ordinary	~~shallow~~	temporary	weak

1 The water's *shallow*. It's only up to my knees.
2 We can't pass that car. The road is too .... .
3 I can't carry your bag. It's too .... .
4 He has a .... job until the end of the summer.
5 It was an .... day, just like every other day.
6 She's very .... because she hasn't eaten for weeks.
7 The cliffs are pretty .... , so they're easy to climb.
8 It's a .... building. It was built two years ago.

5 Write the antonyms of the adjectives in Exercise 4.

shallow – deep

6 Complete the sentences with appropriate words.

1 What stars can you see through a *telescope*?
2 I want to be an a.... and travel in a s.... .
3 Is that a c.... in the sky? Look at its bright tail!
4 Saturn is in the same s.... s.... as Earth.
5 Our g.... has millions of stars.
6 An a.... knows about space, but hasn't been there.

Speaking • Review

7 Complete the conversations with these words. Then listen and check. 3.10

be careful	I were you	~~I wouldn't~~
make sure you	Watch out for	

1 **A** I'm going to swim in the ocean.
B *I wouldn't* swim alone if .... .
2 **A** I'm going shopping.
B OK. But .... don't forget your wallet.
3 **A** I'm going for a bike ride.
B .... the cars. And .... not to stay out after dark.

Dictation

8 Listen and write in your notebook. 3.11

My assessment profile: Workbook page 133

Science File

Asteroids

- **What are asteroids?**
Asteroids are objects in space that are smaller than planets, and that orbit the sun. They are made of rock or metal, and some have ice on them, too. This is the material that wasn't used when the planets in our solar system were formed 4.5 billion years ago.

- **How many asteroids are there in our solar system?**
Millions. Some are small piles of stones, and these are irregular in shape. But the largest asteroid in our solar system, Ceres, is the shape of a planet and has a diameter of 975 km. That's bigger than France!

- **Where are they?**
There are asteroids in many parts of our solar system, but most of them are in the "asteroid belt" between the orbits of Mars and Jupiter.

- **Do asteroids ever crash into planets?**
Yes, sometimes. In fact, some people think that the moon was created when a huge asteroid crashed into Earth early in our planet's history. Another impact event probably caused the extinction of the dinosaurs and other species about 65 million years ago. These big impact events don't happen very often, but smaller rocks strike Earth about 500 times a year. A lot of big holes in the ground were made by these rocks.

- **Is Earth in danger from asteroids today?**
Sometimes big asteroids pass very close to Earth. In 1989 a 300-meter asteroid passed through the exact position where Earth was only six hours before. If an asteroid of that size hit Earth, there would be an explosion twelve times more powerful than a big nuclear bomb. Astronomers think that about 2,000 asteroids bigger than one kilometer might hit Earth in the next billion years. These will be very dangerous. However, there's nothing terrible to worry about until the year 2880, when a kilometer-wide asteroid has a 1 in 300 chance of hitting Earth.

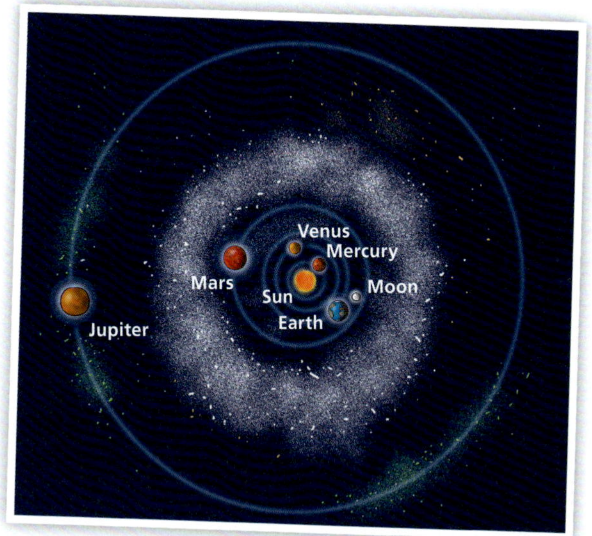

Reading

1 **Read the article quickly. What is the size of the biggest asteroid in our solar system?**

2 (3.12) **Read the article again. Are the statements true (T) or false (F)?**

1 All asteroids are made of rock. *F*
2 Asteroids are many different shapes.
3 Earth's moon used to be an asteroid.
4 An asteroid probably killed the dinosaurs.
5 Rocks from space don't hit Earth very often.
6 A big asteroid will hit Earth in 2880.

Barringer Crater

3 (3.13) **Listen to information about the Barringer Crater. Choose the correct options.**

Where?	[1] *the US* / Australia
When?	[2] *5,000 / 50,000* years ago
What?	a piece of [3] *metal / rock*
How big?	[4] *50 / 300* meters
Results?	• a hole in the ground more than [5] *175 m / 1,200 m* wide • all [6] *plants / animals* in a 1,000 km² area were destroyed

My Science File

4 **Find out about the impact event at either Chicxulub or Tunguska. Make a table about it like the one in Exercise 3.**

5 **Write a short paragraph about the event.**

8 Spies

Grammar
Past perfect;
Third conditional

Vocabulary
Spy collocations;
Adjectives with prefixes *dis-, im-, in-, un-*

Speaking
Explaining and apologizing

Writing
An opinion essay

Word list page 111
Workbook page 111

Vocabulary • Spy collocations

1 3.14 **Match these phrases to the definitions (1–12). Then listen, check and repeat.**

break into somewhere *9*
decode a message
escape from somewhere
follow someone
make a deal
spy on someone
take cover
tap a phone
tell a lie
tell the truth
track down a person
wear a disguise

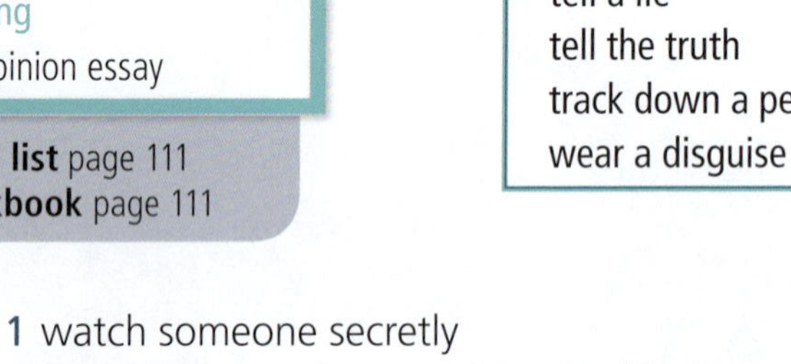

1 watch someone secretly
2 find someone after searching for him/her
3 get away from a dangerous place or situation
4 hide in a place to protect yourself
5 discover the meaning of some secret numbers or letters
6 use equipment to listen to someone's phone calls
7 say the actual facts about something
8 use clothes or other accessories so that people can't recognize you
9 get into a place by using force
10 say something untrue
11 agree to do something in exchange for something else
12 walk or drive secretly behind a person

2 **Look at the picture. Find someone …**

taking cover *3*
tapping a phone
making a deal
wearing a disguise
following another person
breaking into somewhere

3 **Work in pairs. Have you ever done any of the things in Exercise 1? Tell your partner.**

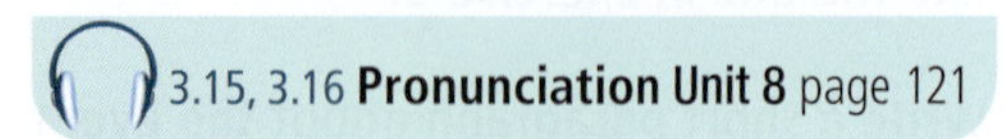
3.15, 3.16 **Pronunciation Unit 8** page 121

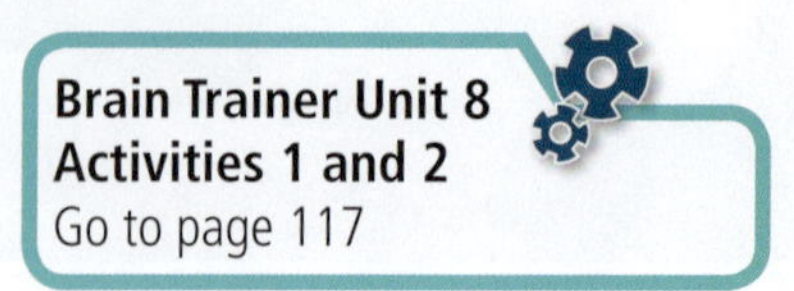
Brain Trainer Unit 8
Activities 1 and 2
Go to page 117

Reading

1 Read the text quickly. Choose the best description.

1 a newspaper article about spies
2 an extract from a spy novel
3 a biography of a famous spy

2 Read the text again and answer the questions.
3.17

1 How did Stella find out where DeVere was?
She decoded a message on her phone.
2 What was Stella probably doing when she "closed her eyes for a brief moment"?
3 How did Stella get from her apartment to Hadrian Avenue?
4 Why didn't DeVere need to wear a disguise?
5 How did DeVere get the virus?
6 How did Stella hide from DeVere?
7 Why did she choose this place to hide?
8 Who said, "... in fact I'm right behind *you*"?

3 What about you? Ask and answer.

1 How was Stella tricked by DeVere? Can you find any clues in the text?
2 What do you think happens next?
3 Do you enjoy reading these kinds of stories? Why?/Why not?

The phone call woke her at seven in the morning. There were no words, just a series of strange noises. Stella listened carefully and wrote some numbers on the notepad beside her phone. By the time she put the pen down, she had already decoded the message. It was an address: 22 Hadrian Avenue. Stella opened a street map, moved her finger along the route, closed her eyes for a brief moment, then raced out of her apartment. As she sped through the empty silver streets on her bike, she reviewed what she already knew about her target. Philip DeVere was an ordinary-looking man. Medium height, medium-brown hair, gray-brown eyes. He didn't need to wear a disguise—his face was instantly forgettable. But this unremarkable man was in fact a very dangerous thief. Before he became a criminal, DeVere had been a brilliant scientist. But then two months ago, he broke into the National School of Tropical Medicine and stole a bottle of a deadly virus. Just one drop could pollute the water supply to an entire city. Stella's job was to track down DeVere and get the virus back.

As she approached Hadrian Avenue, Stella jumped off her bike and took cover behind a blue van parked at the corner. From here she had a good view of the street. Number 22 was an old, gray apartment building across from a small, empty children's playground. In the playground there was a woman with a stroller and an old man sitting on a bench reading a newspaper. Suddenly DeVere came running out of number 22 and across the playground.

Stella had already put her cell phone in her pocket before she left her apartment that morning. Now she took it out and dialed a number. "I'm right behind him," she said. She turned off the phone and put it back in her pocket. "Ah, my dear Stella," said a voice, "but in fact I'm right behind *you*!"

Grammar • Past perfect

By the time she put the pen down, she had already decoded the message.

Before he became a criminal, DeVere had been a brilliant scientist.

Stella had already put her cell phone in her pocket before she left her apartment that morning.

Grammar reference Workbook page 100

Watch Out!

We often use the following time expressions with the Past perfect:

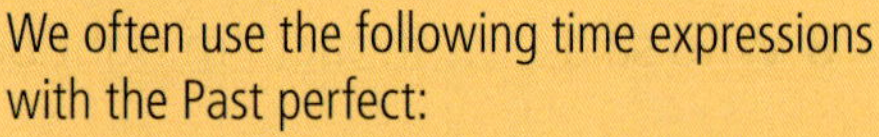

by the time, by (+ a time), just, already, when

By the time Helen finished her call, she had been on the phone for two hours.
The man had just opened the window when there was a loud explosion.

1 Study the grammar table and Watch Out! Choose the correct options to complete the rules.

1 We use the Past perfect to describe an action that occurred *before / after* another action in the past.
2 We form the Past perfect with *has / had* + past participle.

2 Complete the sentences with these words.

buy	get	hear	see	~~send~~	spend

1 I lost the letter that you *had sent* the day before.
2 We .... all our money the weekend before, so we couldn't go out last night.
3 He put on the disguise that he .... at the store the day before.
4 We .... just .... home when the phone rang.
5 I .... never .... that song before you sang it last night.
6 She .... never .... a musical before, and she was very excited.

3 Complete the text with the Past simple or Past perfect form of the verbs.

By the time Stella [1] *was* (be) on her way to Hadrian Avenue, DeVere [2] .... (already/plan) his escape. He [3] .... (put) on his disguise—a white wig and an old coat. He [4] .... (just/pick) up a newspaper when his friend Blaine [5] .... (come) to his door. DeVere [6] .... (give) Blaine his instructions. "Wait five minutes!" he said. "Then run through the playground to the station." Before Blaine [7] .... (have) time to ask any questions, DeVere [8] .... (leave) the building. He [9] .... (walk) slowly to the park bench and [10] .... (start) to read his newspaper. After he [11] .... (wait) for five minutes, he [12] .... (see) Stella turning onto Hadrian Avenue.

4 Put the sentences into the Past perfect.

1 I finished my sandwich, and then I ate a banana. (after)
After I had finished my sandwich, I ate a banana.
2 She opened the window and saw a strange man. (just/when)
3 She put on her coat. Then she left the house. (after)
4 Everyone read the book, and then we discussed it in class. (before).
5 The girl put on her disguise, and then walked into the room. (after)
6 The thief escaped. The alarm bell rang. (already, by the time)

5 Use the Past perfect to make endings to the sentences.

1 When I arrived at the theater *the movie had already started.*
2 When I opened the door …
3 Julie felt sad because …
4 There was no school yesterday because …
5 I was really happy because …

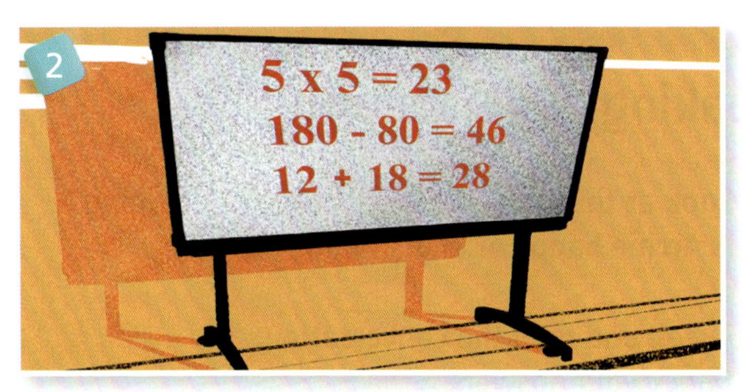

Vocabulary • Adjectives with prefixes *dis-, im-, in-, un-*

1 Match the pictures (1–4) to these adjectives.

dishonest   impossible *1*   incorrect   unfair

2 3.18 **Copy the table. Put the words under the correct headings. Then listen, check your answers and repeat.**

appropriate	~~correct~~	~~fair~~	~~honest~~
important	loyal	patient	polite
~~possible~~	satisfied	successful	tolerant

dis-	im-	in-	un-
dishonest	*impossible*	*incorrect*	*unfair*
....	....	....	....
....	....	....	....

Word list page 111
Workbook page 111

3 Complete the sentences with words from Exercise 2.

1 Our team didn't win the game. We were *unsuccessful*.
2 He said he was sorry, but she was .... with his apology and didn't reply to his letter.
3 This answer is .... . Please look at it again.
4 If you don't support your friends when they have problems, people might think you are .... .
5 This movie is very violent. It's .... for children.
6 My sister never says "please" or "thank you." She's really .... !
7 My dad's boss is very ....—he doesn't like people to disagree with him.
8 You can't get from London to New York in one hour. It's .... !
9 The .... boy cheated on his math exam.
10 I know you think this problem is .... , but it's really worrying me.
11 My sister's piece of cake is much bigger than mine. It's so .... !
12 She's never prepared to wait for other people—she's really .... .

4 What about you? In pairs, tell your partner about

1 a time when you were honest.
2 a time when you felt something was unfair.
3 two situations that make you feel impatient.

Brain Trainer Unit 8
Activity 3
Go to page 117

Chatroom Explaining and apologizing

Speaking and Listening

1 Look at the photo. What is Archie's dad doing? Is Archie happy or angry about this?

2 (3.19) Listen and read the conversation. Check your answers.

3 (3.19) Listen and read again. Answer the questions.

1 Why is Archie's dad looking at Archie's computer?
He wants to check who Archie is talking to online.
2 Does Archie understand that he should be careful about online safety?
3 Why does Archie's dad worry about Archie's online friends?
4 Why does Archie think that this social networking site is safe?
5 Why is Archie so angry with his dad?

4 Act out the conversation in pairs.

Archie What's going on, Dad? Why are you using my computer?
Dad I'm checking your social networking account.
Archie That's uncalled for! You're spying on my private conversations. It's totally unfair.
Dad No, Archie, that's not true. But the fact is that you have to be careful about who you talk to online.
Archie I know that! I would have told you immediately if a stranger had ever tried to contact me online. But nothing like that has ever happened.
Dad I'm sure that's true. But you have to understand that some people can be dishonest about their real identity.
Archie I'm aware of that, Dad. But there's nothing inappropriate on this social networking site. It's approved by my school.
Dad Well, let's forget about it, OK? I'm sorry that I upset you.
Archie OK, whatever. But if you had asked me first, I wouldn't have gotten so angry.

Say it in your language ...
What's going on?
That's uncalled for!

5 **Look at the conversation again. Who says what?**

1 It's totally unfair. *Archie*
2 The fact is that …
3 I know that!
4 I'm sure that's true.
5 You have to understand that …
6 Let's forget about it.

6 **Read the phrases for explaining, acknowledging and apologizing.**

Explaining, acknowledging and apologizing	
Explaining	The fact is that … You have to understand that …
Acknowledging	I know that. I'm aware of that. I'm sure that's true.
Apologizing and accepting an apology	I'm sorry that … Let's forget about it.

7 3.20 **Listen to the conversation. Act out the conversation in pairs.**

Holly Yasmin, why are you [1] using my phone?
Yasmin [2] I'm looking for Fraser's number.
Holly Well, you should ask me first. [3] My phone is private.
Yasmin The fact is that you weren't here, and [4] I need his number now.
Holly I'm sure that's true. But you shouldn't look at other people's stuff without asking.
Yasmin OK, I'm sorry that I upset you.

8 **Work in pairs. Replace the words in purple in Exercise 7. Use these phrases and/or your own ideas. Act out the conversations.**

1 read my diary / in my bedroom / look at my email account
2 want to check when Mark's birthday is / try to find my jacket / look for Sara's email address
3 my diary / my bedroom / my email account
4 organize his party / need my jacket now / want to send her this photo now

Grammar • Third conditional

If you had asked me first, I wouldn't have gotten so angry.
(You didn't ask me first, so I was angry.)

I would have told you immediately if a stranger had tried to contact me.
(A stranger didn't try to contact me, so I didn't tell you.)

Grammar reference Workbook page 100

1 **Study the grammar table. Choose the correct options to complete the rules.**

1 We use the Third conditional to talk about *unreal / real* situations in the past.
2 We form the Third conditional with *if* + *Past perfect / Past participle* + *would(n't) have* + *Past perfect / Past participle*.

2 **Which are the Third conditional (3) sentences?**

1 If I hadn't taken the bus, I would have walked home. *3*
2 If I met Lady Gaga, I would ask for her autograph. ....
3 You wouldn't have failed the test if you had worked harder. ....
4 She would buy a new car if she won $10,000.

3 **Complete the sentences with the correct form of the verbs. Use the Third conditional.**

1 If we *had known* (know) about your party, we *would have gone* (go) to it.
2 If it .... (not rain) yesterday, we .... (play) tennis.
3 If you .... (watch) that horror movie, you .... (be) very scared!
4 Marie .... (practice) the violin this morning if she .... (not hurt) her arm.
5 I .... (help) you if I .... (be) there.

4 **What about you? Write answers to these questions. Use the Third conditional.**

1 Why were you so late yesterday?
I missed the bus. If I hadn't missed the bus, I wouldn't have been late.
2 Why didn't you go to school yesterday?
3 Why did you yell at your friend last night?
4 Why didn't you go swimming last weekend?

Who's Watching You?

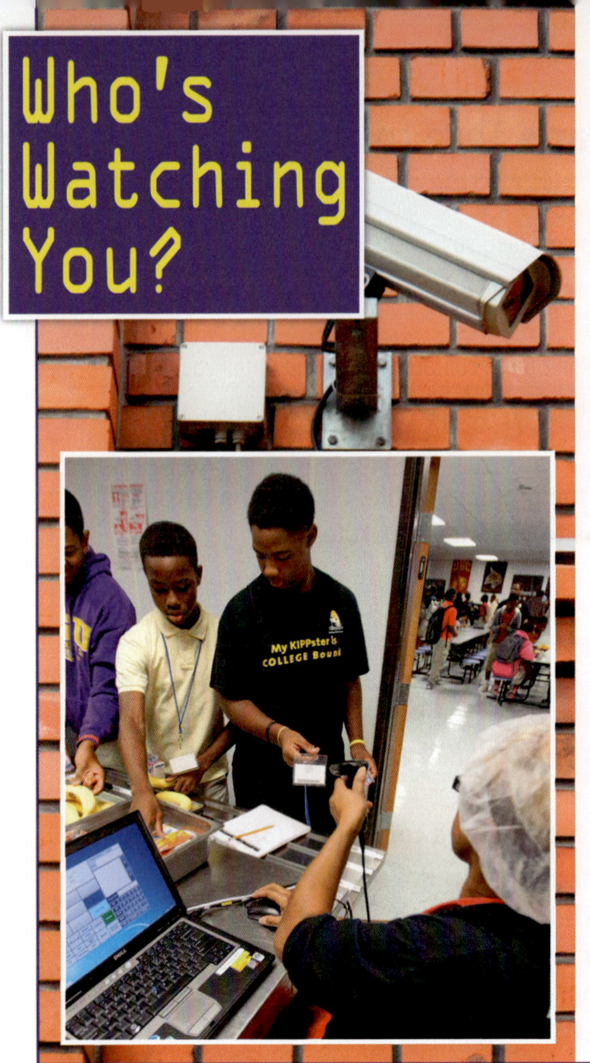

Ted Barnes is a typical 16-year-old student at a large high school in Pittsburgh. He walks to school every morning, attends classes, eats his lunch in the school cafeteria, takes out books from the school library and sometimes goes to an after-school computer club before he walks home. And like most of his classmates, Ted is under surveillance throughout his school day. On his way to school, he walks past four CCTV cameras. Ted's school has thirty CCTV cameras in the hallways and near the school entrance. When Ted checks out books from his library, he uses a fingerprint scanner, and when he buys his lunch in the cafeteria, he uses an ID card, which records what he buys. After school, at computer club, the teacher can see exactly which sites Ted visits and can monitor his online conversations. Ted and many of his friends feel more and more dissatisfied with the level of surveillance in their lives. "Teachers, the police, our parents … they're spying on us all the time. They think that our right to privacy is unimportant," complains Ted. "They don't tap our phones, but they follow us in so many other ways. Nothing is private anymore."

But Andrew Lott, the principal at Ted's school, argues that surveillance is a useful and necessary part of school life. "Before we installed cameras here, students had reported a lot of problems with bullying. We had tried to identify the bullies, but before the CCTV cameras, we were unsuccessful. After we had installed the cameras, we identified the bullies and noticed an immediate improvement in discipline. Now our students know that they are safe at school. If we hadn't put cameras in the hallways, we wouldn't have been able to track down the bullies. It's impossible to have a system that makes everyone happy."

Key Words

surveillance	check out
fingerprint scanner	monitor
privacy	install

Reading

1 **Read the article quickly. Choose the best description of Ted's opinion.**

1 There is too much surveillance in our daily lives.
2 Surveillance is important to keep us safe.
3 We need to find better ways than surveillance to protect students.

2 3.21 **Read the article again. Are these statements true (T), false (F) or don't know (DK)?**

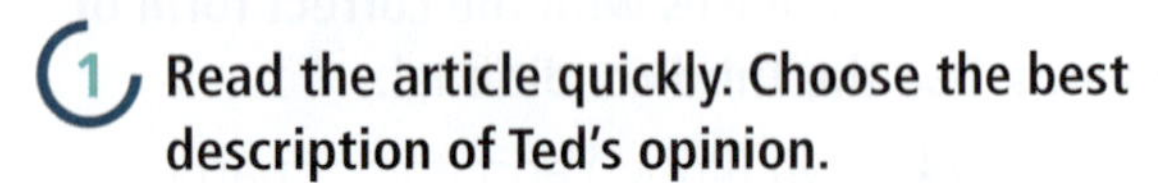

1 Ted is like most other 16-year-old students. *T*
2 Ted goes home at the same time every day.
3 Ted's school can find out what he eats for lunch.
4 There are CCTV cameras in the computer club classroom.
5 Ted thinks that some people are listening to his phone conversations.
6 Andrew Lott agrees with Ted that there is too much surveillance at school.
7 Before CCTV cameras were installed, bullying was the biggest problem at the school.

Listening

1 3.22 **Listen to the interview. How many students does the reporter talk to? Do they agree with each other?**

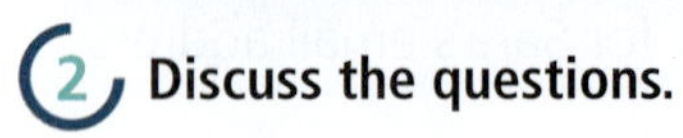

Listening Bank Unit 8 page 120

2 **Discuss the questions.**

1 Do you have CCTV cameras at your school? If so, where are they?
2 Do you think that CCTV cameras can help stop problems like bullying and theft at school?
3 Do you think that CCTV cameras are an invasion of your privacy?

Writing • An opinion essay

1 Read the Writing File.

Writing File Expressing opinions

Introductory paragraph

- **State the topic of the essay and your main opinion.**

Our local council is planning to close the gym and open a new swimming pool. In my opinion,/I think this is an excellent idea.

Middle paragraphs

- **Give reasons for your opinion. Use a new paragraph for each reason.**

In the first place/First, I feel that …
I'm also convinced/I also believe that …
Another point to bear in mind is …
Finally, …

Conclusion

- **State your main opinion again, and give a brief summary of the reasons.**

To conclude, I believe that … because …
In conclusion, my view is that …

2 Put the parts of an essay (a–e) in the correct order.

a In the first place, many parents have already spent a lot of money on the current school uniform this year.
b In conclusion, I am against the introduction of a new school uniform because it will be both more expensive and unpopular.
c Our school wants to introduce a new school uniform. In my opinion, this is a bad idea. *1*
d Finally, the suggested new uniform is much more expensive, and this will affect parents with several children at the school.
e I also believe that our current uniform is very dressy and popular, and most students are proud of it.

3 Read the essay and find the language from the Writing File.

Our school has announced plans to introduce fingerprint scanning in the library. I think this is a really good idea.
In the first place, while it's easy to lose or forget a library card or a PIN, you can't lose your fingers! So students can always take out books when they need to.
I also believe that people can't steal or duplicate fingerprints. Students therefore don't need to worry about other people taking out books in their name.
Although some opponents of the plan think that fingerprint scanning is an invasion of privacy, I'm convinced that they are wrong. The school doesn't store the fingerprints. It converts each fingerprint into a code so no one can steal it or use it.
In conclusion, I believe that fingerprint scanning is a more secure way of borrowing books from the library, and it doesn't threaten students' privacy.

4 Read the essay again and answer the questions.

1 Is the writer for or against fingerprint scanning? *for*
2 How many reasons does the writer give for his/her opinion?
3 What are the advantages of fingerprint scanning?
4 Why does the writer think that fingerprint scanning won't threaten students' privacy?

5 You are going to write an opinion essay. Read the text below. Use ideas from page 94.

Your school is planning to install 45 CCTV cameras in the hallways and classrooms.

- Decide whether you are for or against the plan.
- Plan your paragraphs.
- Include at least three reasons to support your opinion.

6 Now write your opinion essay. Use your ideas from Exercise 5.

Remember!

- Use clear paragraphs and language for giving your opinion.
- Use the vocabulary in this unit.
- Check your grammar, spelling and punctuation.

Refresh Your Memory!

Grammar • Review

1 Complete the sentences with the Past simple or Past perfect form of the verbs.

1 We *had already eaten* (already/eat) lunch before we *went* (go) to the café.
2 By the time I .... (get) to school, the class .... (start).
3 When I .... (arrive) at the movie theater, I .... (see) a long line of people. Some of them .... (be) there for hours, and others .... (just/arrive).
4 I .... (meet) James two years before, but I .... (not/recognize) him when he .... (speak) to me.
5 After she .... (finish) her homework, she .... (watch) TV.
6 We .... (just/open) the window when a bird .... (fly) into the room.

2 Match the beginnings (1–5) to the endings (a–e) of the sentences.

1 If she hadn't pulled the dog's tail, *d*
2 If I hadn't lost my phone,
3 If you had remembered your umbrella,
4 If we had been kinder to her,
5 If you had asked me first,

a I would have called you.
b I would have said yes.
c you wouldn't have gotten so wet.
d it wouldn't have bitten her.
e she wouldn't have been so upset.

3 Make sentences. Use the Third conditional.

1 I didn't remember my books. The librarian was angry.
If I had remembered my books, the librarian wouldn't have been angry.
2 They woke up late. They missed their favorite show on TV.
3 We didn't study for the test. We didn't pass it.
4 She ate a lot of chocolate. She felt sick.
5 Fred and his sister visited their aunt. They didn't go to the football game.
6 I fell asleep during the movie. I didn't understand the ending.

Vocabulary • Review

4 Complete the sentences with the correct form of these words.

break	decode	escape	follow	make	~~spy~~
take	tap	tell (x2)	track	wear	

1 Someone is *spying* on me! A man .... me home yesterday, and I think someone has .... our phone!
2 Can you .... this strange message?
3 OK, I'll .... a deal with you. If you tell me who .... into the school last weekend, I'll give you $50.
4 The police have .... down the dangerous criminal, Harry Thug, who .... from prison last night.
5 Look! It's Tim! He's .... a disguise!
6 Most people don't always .... the truth.
7 I quickly .... cover behind the tree.
8 That girl's .... a lie! I saw her cheat on the exam!

5 Use the prefixes *dis-*, *im-*, *in-* or *un-* to complete the adjectives.

1 *in*appropriate
2 ....correct
3 ....fair
4 ....patient
5 ....important
6 ....honest
7 ....polite
8 ....loyal
9 ....satisfied
10 ....successful

Speaking • Review

6 3.23 **Put the conversation in the correct order. Then listen and check.**

a I know that. But the fact is that I left my wallet on your desk this morning. So maybe you put it in your bag. I'm sorry that I upset you.
b What are you doing with my bag? *1*
c It's not in my bag! And you have to understand that it's important to ask before taking someone's bag.
d OK. Let's forget about it.
e I'm looking for my wallet.

Dictation

7 3.24 **Listen and write in your notebook.**

My assessment profile: Workbook page 134

Marnie Higgins's Profile*

Age	Home country
20	United Kingdom

My favorite things ...

following suspects, taking cover, wearing disguises

Reading

1 Read Marnie's profile and look at the photos. What do you think Marnie's job is?

2 Read the text. Answer the questions.

3.25

1 According to the author, what is the typical image of a private detective?
A middle-aged man wearing a brown coat and a fedora hat.
2 Where does Marnie work?
3 What did Marnie do when she first started working there?
4 Why does Marnie think that young people are better at surveillance?
5 Is the job always dangerous?
6 Why was Marnie's car full of sandwich boxes and magazines?
7 How does Marnie's boss make sure that she is always safe?
8 What does Marnie do now?

*Her photo can't be shown because of her job.

FOLLOW THAT CAR!

When we think of private detectives, we usually imagine middle-aged men dressed in brown coats and wearing fedora hats. But a successful detective agency in southeastern England has a special group of "teen detectives." One of these detectives is Marnie, who started working for the agency while she was still in school. Her first job wasn't as a detective—she was a data entry clerk, but "it was more exciting than stacking shelves in a supermarket!" Marnie explains. One day, one of the other detectives was following a suspect, and he asked Marnie to pretend to be his niece. "I was scared, but it was also really thrilling!" Marnie is now 20 years old, but sometimes she wears a disguise and pretends to be a high school student. "Young people are better at surveillance," she explains. "If you notice a student standing on a street corner, you probably won't suspect she's a private detective!"

But isn't the job very dangerous? "Sometimes it is, but often it's just very boring. When you do surveillance work, you often have to wait in one place for hours and hours. Last week I was in my car outside someone's house for six hours. By the time I had finished, the car was full of magazines, and empty sandwich boxes and soft-drink cans!" Marnie's boss, the head of the detective agency, is careful to protect her safety. "My detectives always wear a 'bug'—a hidden microphone—so that I can follow them and listen to them. If the situation gets dangerous, we step in very quickly." Marnie now combines her detective work with college studies. "Many of the undergraduates in my major have part-time jobs while they study, but I'm the only private detective!"

Class discussion

1 Would you like Marnie's job? Why?/Why not?
2 What would your parents say if you got a job with a detective agency?
3 What personal qualities do you think a private detective needs? Make a list.

Celebrate!

Grammar
Reported statements, commands and requests, questions

Vocabulary
Party collocations; Reporting verbs

Speaking
Reaching an agreement

Writing
A problem page

Word list page 111
Workbook page 112

Vocabulary • Party collocations

1 3.26 **Complete the phrases (1–13) with these words. Then listen, check and repeat.**

do
go
greet
have
hire
make
put up
stay up
~~throw~~
wear (x4)

1 *throw* a party
2 .... a jacket and tie
3 .... dressy clothes
4 .... your hair
5 .... high heels
6 .... decorations
7 .... a DJ
8 .... by limo
9 .... casual clothes
10 .... the time of your life
11 .... all night
12 .... your guests
13 .... a speech

2 Complete the text with words from Exercise 1.

Every year on Oscar night, the world's most famous movie stars [1] *go* by [2] *limo* to the Oscars ceremony in Hollywood. No one wears [3] .... that night. The men wear a [4] .... and [5] .... . The women wear [6] .... clothes too, usually a beautiful long dress and [7] .... on their feet. A professional has done their [8] .... . At the ceremony, each Oscar winner has to [9] .... a [10] .... to say "thank you." Then, after the ceremony, some celebrities [11] .... a [12] .... for their friends. They [13] .... their [14] .... and give them champagne and expensive food. A lot of people [15] .... all [16] .... . No one wants to go to bed when they're having the [17] .... their [18] .... .

3 Describe the photos on this page. Use words from Exercise 1.

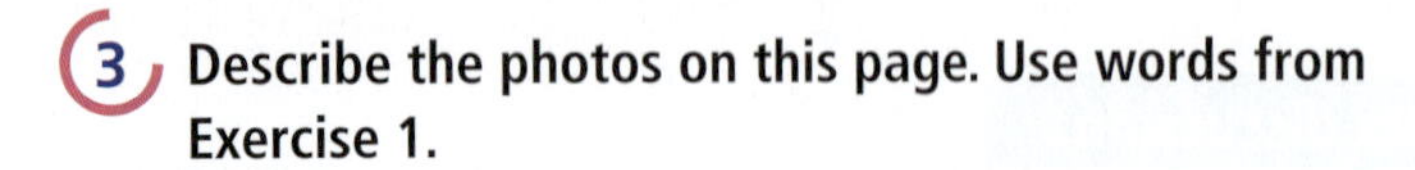

In picture a, they've hired a DJ. Everyone's wearing ...

4 In pairs, ask and answer the questions.

Do you, your family or your friends ever throw parties? What do you do to get ready for them? What do you do at them? What do you wear?

3.27, 3.28 **Pronunciation Unit 9** page 121

Brain Trainer Unit 9
Activities 1 and 2
Go to page 117

Reading

1 Look at the photos and the title. Answer the questions.

1 What are proms?
2 Who goes to them?
3 Which country has them?
4 Is it expensive to go to a prom?

2 Read the article and check your answers to Exercise 1.

3 Read the article again and answer the questions. 3.29

1 What transportation do people use to get to the prom? *They go by limo.*
2 What, according to the article, is wrong with students' ideas for proms?
3 What do people have to pay for if they want to go to a prom?
4 Which teenagers liked the proms at the New View School?
5 Why did some students get weekend jobs?
6 Why were these jobs a problem?
7 What differences are there between the graduation party and a prom?

4 What about you? In pairs, ask and answer.

1 Does your school throw a party for its seniors? What kind of party?
2 Would you like to go to a prom? Why?/Why not?
3 How much money should people spend on a party like a prom? How much is too much?

Prom Night

A prom is a special party for high school seniors, and it's an important tradition in the US. The girls wear a beautiful dress; the boys wear a special evening suit called a tuxedo. They go to the party by limo, which for many is the highlight of their school career.

The average 18-year-old now spends $1,139 on his or her prom night, up from $1,098 last year and $807 the year before. There are the costs of prom tickets, clothes and a limo, and the girls often ask professionals to do their hair, nails and makeup.

Additionally, students always want their prom to be better than the one held the year before. It becomes a kind of competition, and some schools are not happy about this.

"Our school used to have proms in a hotel," says Mr. Turner, principal of the New View School in Phoenix, Arizona. "The richer kids loved them. But others told me they couldn't afford to go. Teachers said that some kids had found weekend jobs to pay for the prom and, as a result, weren't doing enough school work. Finally, we told the students that there wouldn't be any more proms."

Were they disappointed? "Some were, of course. But this year we threw a graduation party in the school auditorium. We told the kids to put up cheap decorations and bring their own music. They wore casual clothes. Everyone felt relaxed, and the kids had the time of their lives."

Grammar • Reported statements

Present simple → Past simple

"Your dress is nice."
→ They said that my dress was nice.

Present continuous → Past continuous

"They aren't doing enough work."
→ He told me that they weren't doing enough work.

Past simple → Past perfect

"The richer kids loved the prom."
→ He told the journalist that the richer kids had loved the prom.

Present perfect → Past perfect

"We have found weekend jobs."
→ They said that they had found weekend jobs.

will → would

"There won't be a prom."
→ We told them that there wouldn't be a prom.

am/is/are going to → was/were going to

"We're going to be there."
→ They told us that they were going to be there.

have to/must → had to

"I must buy a new jacket."
→ He said that he had to buy a new jacket.

can → could

"I can't afford a new car."
→ He told me that he couldn't afford a new car."

Grammar reference Workbook page 102

1 **Study the grammar table. Choose the correct options to complete the rules.**

1 When we report a statement with *said* or *told*, the tense goes *forward / back* in time.
2 There is *always / never* an object after *said*.
3 There is *always / never* an object after *told*.

2 **Complete the sentences. Use reported speech.**

1 "It's a great party."
→ He said that it *was* a great party.
2 "I talked to some nice people."
→ He told me that he .... to some nice people.
3 "I really like Lara."
→ He said that he really .... Lara.
4 "I must see her again."
→ He said that he .... her again.
5 "I've sent her a text message."
→ He told me that he .... her a text message.
6 "I can meet you later."
→ Lara told him that she .... him later.
7 "I'll wait for you at the park."
→ He told Lara that he .... for her at the park.
8 "We're going to go to the movies."
→ He said that they .... to the movies.

Watch Out!

In reported speech, pronouns and place and time expressions sometimes have to change. For example:
now → then
here → there
this week → that week
last month → the month before
next year → the following year

3 **Read the conversation. Then complete the text below. Use reported speech.**

Mia The Fourth of July fireworks are next Tuesday.
Otto I can't think about the Fourth of July now. I'm too busy this week.
Mia You weren't here for July 4 last year. We have to go together this year. It'll be fun.

Mia told Otto that the Fourth of July fireworks were [1] *the following Tuesday*. Otto said that [2] .... couldn't think about the Fourth of July [3] .... because he was too busy [4] .... . Mia said that [5] .... hadn't been [6] .... for July 4 [7] .... . She told him that [8] .... had to go together [9] .... . She said that [10] .... be fun.

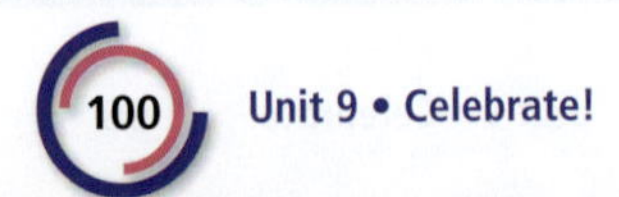

• Reported commands and requests

"Put up decorations."
→ I told you to put up decorations.

"Can you do our hair, please?"/"Please do our hair."
→ They asked her to do their hair.

"Don't hire a DJ."
→ He told us not to hire a DJ.

Grammar reference Workbook page 102

1 Study the grammar box. Choose the correct options.

1 When we are reporting a command or request, we use the *infinitive* / *-ing* form.
2 In the negative, we use *don't* / *not* + infinitive.
3 We *use* / *don't use* "please" in reported requests.

2 Make commands and requests. Use reported speech.

1 "Please eat some food." (He asked us …)
He asked us to eat some food.
2 "Don't cancel the party." (She told him …)
3 "Don't worry about the noise." (They told her …)
4 "Could you help with the decorations?" (She asked me …)
5 "Don't wear casual clothes." (They told us …)

3 Work in pairs. Give your partner a command. Your partner does the action and reports what you have said.

Touch your ear with your hand!

4 Make sentences. Use commands, requests or statements in reported speech.

1 "We're going to cook sausages tonight."
→ They told her *that they were going to cook sausages that night.*
2 "Don't forget the bread."
→ I told him …
3 "I've always loved watching fireworks."
→ She said …
4 "Please come to my Halloween party."
→ She asked me …
5 "It'll be fun."
→ She told me …

Vocabulary • Reporting verbs

1 3.30 **Match the verbs in bold in the sentences (1–10) to the definitions (a–j). Then listen, check and repeat.**

1 She **admitted** that she'd broken my laptop. *d*
2 He **agreed** to do the vacuuming.
3 They **complained** that the music was terrible.
4 She **explained** that a "paw paw" is a type of fruit.
5 We **invited** him to go on vacation with us.
6 He **mentioned** that he had seen you at the party.
7 She **offered** to bring some food. She's so kind.
8 We **promised** to take care of him.
9 I **refused** to help him. He can do it himself.
10 He **warned** us not to make a mess.

a give information so someone can understand it
b tell someone that you will definitely do something
c talk about something during a conversation
d agree that something is true
e ask someone to come to an event with you
f say that you won't do something
g say yes to an idea or plan
h say that you are happy to do something helpful
i tell someone that something bad might happen
j say that you are annoyed about something

Word list page 111 **Workbook** page 112

2 Which pattern do the verbs in Exercise 1 follow? What about *say*, *tell* and *ask*?

1 verb + object (+ *not*) + infinitive *invite, …*
2 verb (+ *not*) + infinitive
3 verb + *that* + reported statement

3 Complete the sentences. Use the structures from Exercise 2.

1 "I'm not going to do it." He refused *to do it*.
2 "My leg hurts." She complained … .
3 "Have dinner with me, Lulu." He invited … .
4 "Don't be late, children." She warned … .
5 "OK, I'll write to her." I agreed … .
6 "I forgot about the party." She admitted … .
7 "It's my birthday soon." He mentioned … .
8 "We'll carry the boxes." They offered … .
9 "I can't afford the ticket." She explained … .
10 "I won't tell anyone." She promised … .

Brain Trainer Unit 9 Activity 3
Go to page 117

Chatroom Reaching an agreement

Speaking and Listening

1 Look at the photo. Answer the questions.

1 What are the friends wearing?
2 Where are they going?
3 Why are they riding bikes?

2 3.31 **Listen and read the conversation. Check your answers.**

3 3.31 **Listen and read again. Answer the questions.**

1 Who booked the limo? *Archie*
2 Why does Archie make a phone call?
3 Why hasn't the limo driver arrived yet?
4 When is he going to arrive?
5 Why doesn't Yasmin want to walk to school?
6 Why do they decide to go by bike?

4 Act out the conversation in groups of four.

Yasmin Hey, Archie, what color is our limo for the prom?
Archie I don't know. I asked how much it was, but I didn't ask about the color. The driver agreed to be here by seven. What time is it now?
Fraser Seven fifteen. Why don't we call him?
Archie That's a good idea. I'll go and call now. (*Later*) Oh man. I asked him if he was almost here, and he admitted that he'd forgotten all about us!
Holly Is he coming now?
Archie No, he said he couldn't come.
Yasmin But that's a disaster!
Fraser It's not the end of the world. Do you think we could walk to school?
Yasmin No way! I'm wearing high heels.
Holly Then I think we should go by bike. We can get to school pretty quickly that way.
Archie That makes sense. Come on, everyone!

Say it in your language ...
That's a disaster!
It's not the end of the world.

5 **Look back at the conversation. Who says what?**

1 Why don't we call him? *Fraser*
2 That's a good idea.
3 Do you think we could walk to school?
4 No way!
5 I think we should go by bike.
6 That makes sense.

6 **Read the phrases for reaching an agreement.**

Making suggestions
Do you think we could …?
I think we should …
Maybe we can …
Why don't we …?

Agreeing	Disagreeing
That's a good idea. That makes sense.	I don't think we should … No way!

7 3.32 **Listen to the conversations. What do the speakers agree to do? Act out the conversations.**

Yasmin [1] We've run out of food.
Holly Why don't we [2] walk to the store?
Yasmin No way! [3] It's raining.
Holly Do you think we could [4] ask Archie to get some chips from his house?
Yasmin That's a good idea. Let's do that.

Archie [1] There aren't any tickets for Saturday.
Fraser Maybe we can [2] go on Sunday.
Archie I don't think we should do that. [3] It'll end late, and we'll have school the next day.
Fraser Then I think we should [4] go on Friday.
Archie That makes sense. OK.

8 **Work in pairs. Replace the words in purple in Exercise 7. Use these words and/or your own ideas. Act out the conversations.**

1 It's her birthday tomorrow. / The buses are canceled. / We need a DJ for the party.

2 throw her a party / go by bike / hire someone

3 It's too late. / It's too far. / DJs are expensive.

4 make her a birthday card / ask your mom to drive us / ask my brother to be the DJ

Grammar • Reported questions

Wh questions
"How much is it?" → I asked how much it was.
"Where were you?" → She asked me where I'd been.

yes/no questions
"Do you like my dress?" → She asked him if he liked her dress.
"Will they bike to the party?" → We asked if they would bike to the party.

Grammar reference Workbook page 102

1 **Study the grammar table. Choose the correct options to complete the rules.**

1 The word order in reported questions is the same as in an ordinary *question / statement*.
2 We *use / don't use do, does* and *did*.
3 The tense in the reported question *changes / doesn't change*.
4 We introduce a *yes/no* reported question with *if / that*.

2 **Make the questions into reported questions.**

1 "Where are you going, Mike?" asked Suzie.
Suzie asked Mike where he was going.
2 "Kate, have you seen Millie?" I asked.
3 "What did you wear to the prom?" she asked me.
4 "Ben, will you be in Seattle tomorrow?" they asked.

3 **Read the conversation. Then complete the text below. Use reported questions.**

Dan Hey, Joy! Great party! Who's the girl with short dark hair?
Joy She's my friend Ella's sister.
Dan Does she go to our school?
Joy No, she goes to school in San Francisco.
Dan Uh … Does she have a boyfriend?
Joy I don't know.
Dan Can you please find out for me?

Dan asked Joy [1] *who the girl with short dark hair was*, and Joy told him [2] .... . Dan asked her [3] .... , and Joy said [4] .... . After that, he asked Joy [5] .... . When Joy said [6] .... , Dan asked her [7] .... for him.

Reading

1 Look at the title and the photos. What is happening in each one? Match three of the photos to the countries (1–3).

1 Taiwan
2 Mexico
3 Brazil

Coming of Age

We asked young people around the world what made them an adult in their country. Here are some of the most fascinating answers that we received.

Huang | Taiwan

In my country, we have a special ceremony for all sixteen-year-olds. I did the ceremony last year. Before it, my mother explained the traditions. She said that the goddess Chiniangma had taken care of me for the first sixteen years of my life, but now I had to share the adult responsibilities in the family. At the beginning of the ceremony, I had to wash my hands in a special bowl, as a sign that I was washing away my old habits. Then I had to crawl under a wooden pagoda that my parents were holding. This was my journey into adult life.

Nerea | Mexico

Girls in Mexico become adults on their fifteenth birthday. Their parents throw a big party called *quince años*. First, you go to church, and after that, all the guests meet in a hotel. Traditionally, this party is the first time that a Mexican girl dances in public, and the first time that she puts on makeup. In the middle of the party, the girl's father takes off her flat shoes and puts high heels on her feet, as a sign that she's now a woman.

Bruno | Brazil

As in Mexico, girls in Brazil have a big party when they are fifteen. But some tribes in the Brazilian rain forest have much scarier traditions. The boys of the Satere-Mawe tribe have to put their hands into gloves full of poisonous ants for ten minutes. I saw a TV show about it, and it said that each ant sting hurt thirty times more than a wasp sting. The boys have to do this glove ceremony twenty times to become an adult!

Key Words

ceremony crawl pagoda
flat ants sting
wasp

2 Read the article quickly and check your ideas.

3 Read the article again. Which country has coming-of-age ceremonies … (3.33)

1 for a) girls? *Mexico* b) boys and girls?
2 for people age a) fifteen? b) sixteen?
3 that involve a) water? b) animals?

4 Read the article again. Answer the questions. (3.33)

1 How did Huang learn about the meaning of his ceremony? *from his mother*
2 What was the meaning of his crawl under the wooden pagoda?
3 According to Mexican tradition, what two things shouldn't girls do before they are fifteen?
4 What change happens during a *quince años* party?
5 Where does the Satere-Mawe tribe live?
6 Why is the glove ceremony scary?

Listening

1 Look at photo c and listen to a radio interview. Answer the questions. (3.34)

1 What country is this?
2 How old are the girls in the photo?
3 What have they done today?

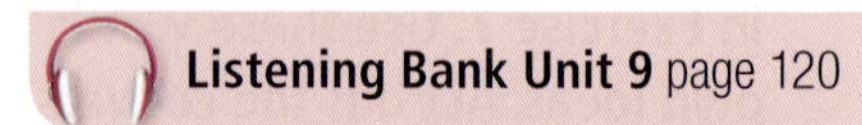
Listening Bank Unit 9 page 120

2 What about you? Ask and answer the questions in pairs.

1 How old are people in your country when they become adults? Do you think it is the right age?
2 Are there any coming-of-age traditions in your country? Describe them.
3 What do you think of the ceremonies in the pictures? Which of them would you like to experience, and which not? Why?

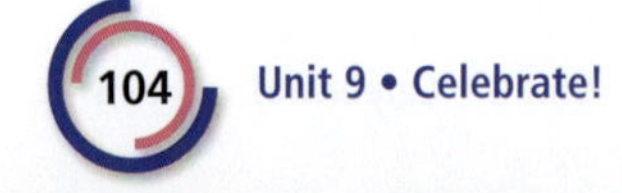

Writing • A problem page

1 **Read the Writing File.**

Writing File Referencing

Try not to repeat the same nouns too often in your writing. Use pronouns and possessive adjectives instead.

- I like parties. ~~Parties~~ They *are fun.*
- *It's Mark's birthday. I'm giving* ~~Mark~~ him *a T-shirt.*
- *Lia's dress is nice, and* ~~Lia's~~ her *shoes are cool, too.*

2 **Read part of a problem page in a magazine. What nouns do the underlined words replace?**

Problem Page

Dear Amy,

It's my birthday next week and I've asked four of my friends to go out for dinner with me. Last week [1] they *my friends* all said that they could go, but this morning three of [2] them told me that they had made other plans. I'm really upset. Should I cancel my birthday dinner, or have [3] it with the one friend who is still free?

Matt

Dear Matt,

I'm sorry to hear about your problem. It is often hard to organize parties and birthday celebrations!

Did you ask your friends why they had changed [4] their plans? They probably had a good reason. For example, maybe your dinner finishes late on a school night, and their parents told them that [5] they couldn't go to [6] it. Or maybe they had already promised to do something else before you invited them, but they had forgotten about [7] it. If their reason is good enough, you should arrange your dinner for a night that is easier for everyone. However, it's possible that these people don't really want to be at your dinner. If that is true, you should have [8] it without [9] them. One real friend is better than a group of false friends, in my opinion.

Good luck. I hope you have the time of your life on your birthday. Relax and enjoy [10] it!

Amy

3 **Read Amy's answer again and answer the questions.**

1 How does she feel about the problem?
2 What three possible reasons for the problem does she mention?
3 What two solutions does she suggest?
4 What final advice does she give?

4 **Read the problem. What do you think the solution is?**

Dear Amy,

Last week my mom said that I could have a birthday party at my house, but now she's changed her mind. The problem is that I've already invited all my friends. What should I do? It'll be terrible if I cancel the party.

Charlotte

5 **Match the reasons (1–5) to the solutions (a–e).**

1 Mom is worried about the noise. *e*
2 Mom is too busy.
3 Mom is worried about the mess.
4 Mom thinks you're not reliable enough.
5 Mom thinks you'll stay up all night.

a Change the date of the party.
b Have the party in the backyard or at a park.
c Promise to end the party early.
d Say that there won't be any bad behavior.
e Promise not to play loud music.

6 **Write a reply to the problem. Use the questions in Exercise 3, the ideas from Exercise 5 and the outline below to help you.**

Paragraph 1
Express sympathy with the writer.
Paragraph 2
Discuss some reasons for the problem and some possible solutions.
Paragraph 3
End with some positive words and some final advice.

Remember!

- Use pronouns and possessive adjectives so you don't repeat nouns too often.
- Use vocabulary and grammar from this unit.
- Check your grammar, spelling and punctuation.

Refresh Your Memory!

Grammar • Review

1 Make sentences. Use reported speech.

1 "I am from Venice, Italy." (She said ...)
She said she was from Venice, Italy.
2 "I loved the carnival last year." (She told me ...)
3 "I've never seen such great fireworks." (She said ...)
4 "I'll send you some photos." (She told me ...)
5 "We're going to invite a lot of friends next year." (She said ...)
6 "I hope you can come, too." (She told me ...)

2 Complete the text with the correct form of these verbs.

~~buy~~	cook	go	not complain
not give	play	ride	

In the morning, Mom asked me [1] *to buy* some pizzas on the way home from school. But after school, my friend asked me [2] .... soccer with him, and I forgot about the pizzas. When I got home, Mom asked me [3] .... my bike to the store, but I told her [4] .... me all the jobs. She got angry and told me [5] .... to my room. Later, I said that I was hungry and asked her [6] .... something, but she told me [7] .... . It's nine o'clock, and I haven't eaten anything since lunch!

3 Make reported questions.

1 "When are the guests arriving?" he asked.
He asked when the guests were arriving.
2 "Why did Sam get here late?" he asked.
3 "Did he bring any food?" we asked.
4 "Do I have to wear a tie?" he asked.
5 "Can I choose the music?" she asked.
6 "What time are we going to leave?" I asked.

4 Put the text into reported speech.

"Where are you, Sophie?" asked Connor.
Connor asked Sophie where she was.
"Hurry up!" he told her. "The prom is starting soon."
"I haven't done my hair," said Sophie. Then she asked, "Are my high heels in the hall?"
Connor looked. "They aren't here," he said, "and it's already six fifteen."
"Go without me," said Sophie. "I'll come later."
"Don't worry," said Connor. "I'm happy to wait."

Vocabulary • Review

5 Complete the text with these words.

all night	casual clothes	decorations
DJ	dressy clothes	hair
high heels	jacket and tie	limo
~~party~~	time of our lives	

My friends and I are going to throw a [1] *party* this July. We've hired a [2] .... for the music, and we're going to put up a lot of [3] .... . Everyone's going to wear [4] .... : a [5] .... for the boys, and a dress and [6] .... for the girls. If anyone wears [7] .... , they won't be allowed into the party. My friends and I are going to do our [8] .... at my house. We're going to go to the party by [9] .... . We're planning to stay up [10] .... , and I'm sure we'll have the [11] .... .

6 Complete the sentences with these verbs.

admitted	complained	offered
promised	~~refused~~	warned

1 He was tired, so he *refused* to go running with us.
2 We .... that the school food tasted awful.
3 They .... to come, so why aren't they here?
4 I .... you not to touch that dog. It bites.
5 She .... that she had cheated on the exam.
6 I .... to help her, but she didn't want any help.

Speaking • Review

7 Put the conversation in the correct order. Then listen and check. 3.35

a That makes sense. Who can we ask?
b Why don't we go to the store and buy some more?
c We don't have enough decorations. *1*
d I think we should ask Katie. Her parents have a lot of useful things in their attic.
e That's a good idea. Let's go to her house now!
f Maybe we can borrow some.
g No way! We can't afford any more.

Dictation

8 Listen and write in your notebook. 3.36

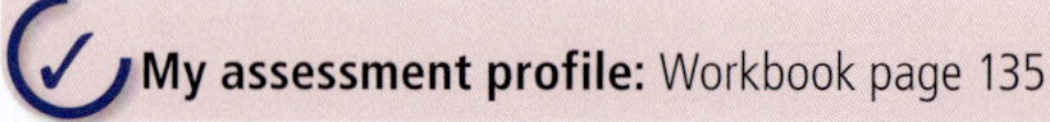
My assessment profile: Workbook page 135

History File

Oliver Cromwell

These days Britain is one of the few countries in the world with a king or queen. 360 years ago, however, there wasn't a royal ruler in Britain. Instead, there was Oliver Cromwell.

Cromwell was an ordinary farmer until he decided to become a politician at the age of 40. The king at that time was Charles I. Cromwell and the other politicians in Parliament kept complaining that his taxes were unfair, but Charles refused to listen. In 1642 a civil war started between Parliament and the king. Cromwell became the leader of the Parliamentarian soldiers. After many years, Parliament won the war and put Charles I in prison. In 1649 the king was executed.

Oliver Cromwell was now the most powerful person in England, and in 1653 he started ruling the country without help from Parliament. He was a Puritan, a type of Christian who believed that people should work very hard, and that having fun was a sin. Under Cromwell, England had some very strict rules. No one could wear makeup, jewelry or colorful dresses. Theaters were closed, and most sports were illegal. In the time of Charles I, people used to celebrate holy days with special food and dancing. Under Cromwell, they celebrated these days by eating no food all day. On Christmas Day, soldiers walked around towns and cities. If they found any special Christmas food or decorations, they took them away. Most people hated living in Cromwell's England.

After Cromwell died in 1658, Charles I's son, Charles II, was invited to rule England. When the new king arrived from Holland, there were huge celebrations around the country. His journey through London to his palace took seven hours because there were so many happy people in the streets. Charles II soon canceled Cromwell's strict rules. The people of England were relieved that Cromwell was gone.

Reading

1 **Read the text quickly. Complete the fact file.**

FACT FILE

Name:	[1] *Oliver Cromwell*
Country:	[2] ....
Early career:	He was a [3] .... and then a [4] .... .
Ruled:	from [5] .... to [6] ....
During his rule:	strict [7] .... about clothes, food and entertainment

2 **Read the text again. Answer the questions.** 3.37

1 Why was Charles I an unpopular king?
Because he made people pay unfair taxes.
2 What religious beliefs did Cromwell have?
3 What rules did Cromwell have about a woman's appearance?
4 How were holy days different under Charles I and Cromwell?
5 How did people feel when Charles II became king?

3 **Listen to the people. Who are they talking about? Copy and complete the table.** 3.38

a Charles I b Cromwell c Charles II

1	c	4	....
2	....	5	....
3	....	6	....

My History File

4 **Find out about another important ruler. Make a fact file like the one in Exercise 1.**

5 **Prepare a presentation for the class about this ruler, including pictures if possible. Then give your presentation.**

Grammar • First and Second conditional

1 Match the beginnings of the sentences (1–7) to the endings (a–g).

1 If you eat too much chocolate, — c
2 If you won the lottery,
3 If you don't hurry up,
4 If you lost your mom's phone,
5 If you pass this exam,
6 If you saw a ghost,
7 If you were late for school,

a she'd be so angry.
b your teacher wouldn't be happy.
c you'll feel sick.
d would you give me some money?
e you'll miss the bus.
f you'll be glad.
g would you be scared?

2 Complete the sentences. Use the correct form of the verbs.

1 Would you buy that bike if you *had* (have) enough money?
2 If you .... (leave) now, you'll get there tonight.
3 I .... (not/be) angry if you tell me the truth.
4 If we moved to France, we .... (learn) French.
5 I .... (not/do) that if I were you.
6 She'll get wet if she .... (not/have) an umbrella.

• Subject/Object questions

3 Are these subject questions (S) or object questions (O)?

1 What do you do all day? *O*
2 What happens on Christmas Day?
3 Who sent me this text?
4 Who did she send this text to?

4 Make a subject and an object question for each sentence.

1 Joe gave the book to Penny. (Who/What)
Who gave the book to Penny?
What did Joe give to Penny?
2 Penny read the book. (Who/What)
3 Henry usually goes to the movies on Sunday. (Who/When)
4 My friends live near the school. (Who/Where)
5 The small brown dog jumped through the window. (Which dog/Where)

• Past perfect

5 Put these sentences into the Past perfect.

1 I saw him before.
I had seen him before.
2 We watched the movie several months ago.
3 She drove there yesterday.
4 My friends returned from Seattle last Tuesday.
5 She went to the station before breakfast.
6 He wrote to me last summer.

6 Complete the text with the Past perfect or Past simple form of the verbs.

By the time I [1] *got* (get) to my apartment, Rose [2] .... (already/disappear). I [3] .... (turn) around and [4] .... (run) down the stairs. Before Rose [5] .... (go), she [6] .... (leave) a note for me on the kitchen table. It was a poem. Rose [7] .... (write) it several months earlier. But I [8] .... (not/understand) it.

• Third conditional

7 Complete the Third conditional sentences.

1 If you *had warned* (warn) me, I *wouldn't have answered* (not answer) the door.
2 If I .... (read) the book, I .... (understand) the movie better.
3 If she .... (not smile) at him, he .... (feel) so sad.
4 You .... (not miss) the train if you .... (run) faster.
5 She .... (buy) the bag if it .... (be) cheaper.
6 If they .... (forget) the tickets, they .... (not get) into the concert.

8 Make sentences. Use the Third conditional.

1 Sarah didn't buy any food, so she felt hungry.
If Sarah had bought some food, she wouldn't have felt hungry.
2 Richard practiced the piano, and he passed his exam.
3 Jade forgot her phone, so she didn't get her friend's message.
4 Frances and Anna didn't join the drama club, so they didn't perform in the play.
5 You fell and hurt your knee.
6 My aunt's car broke down, so she was late for work.

• Reported statements

9 Make these sentences into reported statements. Begin each statement with *He said that …*

1 "She loves coffee, but she hates tea."
He said that she loved coffee, but she hated tea.
2 "They've never been to Japan."
3 "We are studying history this afternoon."
4 "She didn't bike to school."
5 "I am going to meet my friends, and we will probably go to the movies."
6 "You can read the book, but you must give it back to me."

• Reported commands and requests

10 Complete the reported commands and requests.

1 "Open the door!" (She told me …)
She told me to open the door.
2 "Don't stand on the chair!" (He told her …)
3 "Could you make me a sandwich?" (She asked him …)
4 "Can you buy me a new phone?" (He asked them …)
5 "Don't read your book!" (They told her …)
6 "Give the letter to your teacher." (She told him …)

• Reported questions

11 Make reported questions.

1 me why / She asked / in her yard. / I was
She asked me why I was in her yard.
2 her what / she was doing. / He asked
3 them if / He asked / his dog. / they had found
4 us where / the movie theater was. / She asked
5 watching TV. / I asked / they were / them if

12 Make these questions into reported questions. Begin each question with *He asked me …*

1 "Have you ever written a poem?"
He asked me if I had ever written a poem.
2 "Is your friend feeling OK?"
3 "When are you going to have lunch?"
4 "Will your team win the game?"
5 "Can you swim faster than Sharon?"

Speaking • Giving warnings

1 Choose the correct options to complete the conversation.

A I [1] *wouldn't / won't* go swimming in the ocean today if I [2] *were / be* you.
B Why not? I swim in the ocean every day.
A Well, watch [3] *out / about* for the jellyfish on the beach. [4] *Make / Do* sure you don't step on them.
B OK.
A And [5] *be / take* careful not to swim too close to the speedboats.
B Mom! Stop worrying! I'll be fine.

• Explaining and apologizing

2 Complete the conversation with these words.

have to understand	~~I know~~	I'm aware
let's forget	sorry that	that's true
the fact		

A What are you doing in my bedroom?
B I want to borrow your pink jacket.
A Well, you should ask before coming into my room.
B [1] *I know* that. But [2] .... is that you were busy, and I'm going out soon.
A I'm sure [3] .... . But it's no excuse.
B So, can I borrow your jacket?
A No, you can't! You [4] .... that my stuff is mine.
B [5] .... of that. I'm [6] .... I upset you.
A OK, [7] .... about it.

• Reaching an agreement

3 Complete the conversation.

A Mom's really upset. We forgot her birthday!
B Oh no! [1] W*hy* d*on't* we make a cake for her right now?
A [2] I d_ _ '_ t_ _nk we s_ _ _ld do that. We'll just make a mess in the kitchen.
B [3] M_ _b_ we c_ _ go out now and buy her some chocolates.
A [4] N_ w_ _! She hates chocolate.
B [5] D_ you t_ _nk we c_ _ld order some flowers for her?
A [6] T_ _ _'s a g_ _d i_ _ _. She loves flowers.

Vocabulary • Adjective antonyms

1 Complete the antonyms of these adjectives with the missing letters.

1 high — *low*
2 modern — an _ _ _nt
3 narrow — w_ _e
4 ordinary — st_ _ _ _e
5 weak — p_ _ _rful / st_ _ _g
6 deep — s_ _ll_ _
7 light — h_ _v_ / d_ _k
8 permanent — t_ _por_ _ _

• Space

2 Match these words to the definitions (1–8).

asteroid astronomer comet ~~galaxy~~
orbit planet spacecraft star

1 a very large group of stars and planets *galaxy*
2 a large rock that moves around in space
3 a bright object in space
4 the path of an object that moves around another object in space
5 a large round object that moves around a sun or a star
6 a person who studies planets, stars and space
7 a vehicle for traveling through space
8 an object that looks like a star with a tail

• Spy collocations

3 Choose the correct options.

1 *tap* / *decode* a phone
2 *tell* / *make* a lie
3 *decode* / *track down* a person
4 *follow* / *spy* on someone
5 *make* / *wear* a deal
6 *break into* / *decode* a message
7 *tap* / *wear* a disguise
8 *follow* / *break into* a place
9 *take* / *tap* cover
10 *follow* / *decode* a person
11 *break into* / *tell* the truth
12 *escape* / *break* from somewhere

• Adjectives with prefixes *dis-*, *im-*, *in-* and *un-*

4 Put the letters in the correct order to complete the adjectives.

1 r i a f — un*fair*
2 c c s u u l e s f s — un....
3 y o l a l — dis....
4 n e o h s t — dis....
5 p r a t i o p a p r e — in....
6 r c r c o t e — in....
7 t i a p e n t — im....
8 t i l p e o — im....

• Party collocations

5 Complete the text with these words.

dressy greeted heels hired hair
jacket limo put up ~~throw~~ time

Last weekend we decided to [1] *throw* a party for all our friends. We [2] .... a lot of decorations and [3] .... a DJ. We asked everyone to wear [4] .... clothes—a [5] .... and tie for the boys and dresses with high [6] .... for the girls. We spent a long time doing our [7] .... . Some of our friends even went to the party by [8] .... . We stood at the door and [9] .... all our guests. It was amazing, and we all had the [10] .... of our lives!

• Reporting verbs

6 Choose the correct options to complete the text.

Jane [1] *refused* / *offered* to speak to Patrick because he had stolen $5 from her wallet. Patrick [2] *admitted* / *warned* that he had taken the money, but [3] *agreed* / *explained* that he had planned to give it back. He [4] *mentioned* / *promised* to give the $5 back to Jane by the end of the week. But at the end of the week, Jane [5] *complained* / *invited* that she still hadn't received the money. She [6] *warned* / *admitted* Patrick that she would tell his parents. We all [7] *promised* / *agreed* that Patrick had made a big mistake.

Word list

Unit 7 • Final Frontiers

Adjective antonyms

ancient	/ˈeɪnʃənt/
dark	/dɑrk/
deep	/dip/
heavy	/ˈhevi/
high	/haɪ/
light	/laɪt/
low	/loʊ/
modern	/ˈmɑdɚn/
narrow	/ˈnæroʊ/
ordinary	/ˈɔrdnˌeri/
permanent	/ˈpɚmənənt/
powerful	/ˈpaʊɚfəl/
shallow	/ˈʃæloʊ/
strange	/streɪndʒ/
strong	/strɔŋ/
temporary	/ˈtempəˌreri/
weak	/wik/
wide	/waɪd/

Space

asteroid	/ˈæstəˌrɔɪd/
astronaut	/ˈæstrəˌnɔt/
astronomer	/əˈstrɑnəmɚ/
comet	/ˈkɑmɪt/
galaxy	/ˈgæləksi/
moon	/mun/
orbit	/ˈɔrbɪt/
planet	/ˈplænət/
solar system	/ˈsoʊlɚ ˌsɪstəm/
spacecraft	/ˈspeɪskræft/
star	/stɑr/
telescope	/ˈteləskoʊp/

Unit 8 • Spies

Spy collocations

break into somewhere	/ˌbreɪk ˈɪntə ˈsʌmwer/
decode a message	/dɪˌkoʊd ə ˈmesɪdʒ/
escape from somewhere	/ɪˈskeɪp frəm ˈsʌmwer/
follow someone	/ˈfɒloʊ ˌsʌmwʌn/
make a deal	/ˌmeɪk ə ˈdil/
spy on someone	/ˈspaɪ ɔn ˌsʌmwʌn/
take cover	/ˌteɪk ˈkʌvɚ/
tap a phone	/ˌtæp ə ˈfoʊn/
tell a lie	/ˌtel ə ˈlaɪ/
tell the truth	/ˌtel ðə ˈtruθ/
track down a person	/ˌtræk ˈdaʊn ə ˈpɚsən/
wear a disguise	/ˌwer ə dɪsˈgaɪz/

Adjectives with prefixes *dis-*, *im-*, *in-* and *un-*

dishonest	/dɪsˈɑnɪst/
disloyal	/dɪsˈlɔɪəl/
dissatisfied	/dɪˈsætəsˌfaɪd/
impatient	/ɪmˈpeɪʃənt/
impolite	/ˌɪmpəˈlaɪt/
impossible	/ɪmˈpɑsəbəl/
inappropriate	/ˌɪnəˈproʊpri-ət/
incorrect	/ˌɪnkəˈrekt/
intolerant	/ɪnˈtɑlərənt/
unfair	/ˌʌnˈfer/
unimportant	/ˌʌnɪmˈpɔrtnt/
unsuccessful	/ˌʌnsəkˈsesfəl/

Unit 9 • Celebrate!

Party collocations

do your hair	/ˌdu yɚ ˈheər/
go by limo	/goʊ baɪ ˈlɪmoʊ/
greet your guests	/ˌgrit yɚ ˈgests/
have the time of your life	/ˌhæv ðə ˈtaɪm əv yɚ ˈlaɪf/
hire a DJ	/ˌhaɪɚ ə ˈdi ˈdʒeɪ/
make a speech	/ˌmeɪk ə ˈspitʃ/
put up decorations	/ˌpʊt ʌp ˌdekəˈreɪʃənz/
stay up all night	/ˌsteɪ ˌʌp ˈɔl ˈnaɪt/
throw a party	/ˌθroʊ ə ˈpɑrti/
wear a jacket and tie	/ˌwer ə ˈdʒækɪt ən ˈtaɪ/
wear casual clothes	/ˌwer ˈkæʒuəl ˈkloʊðz/
wear dressy clothes	/ˌwer ˈdresi ˈkloʊðz/
wear high heels	/ˌwer ˈhaɪ ˈhilz/

Reporting verbs

admit	/ədˈmɪt/
agree	/əˈgri/
complain	/kəmˈpleɪn/
explain	/ɪkˈspleɪn/
invite	/ɪnˈvaɪt/
mention	/ˈmenʃən/
offer	/ˈɔfɚ/
promise	/ˈprɑmɪs/
refuse	/rɪˈfyuz/
warn	/wɔrn/

Brain Trainers

Unit 1

1 Look at the pieces of paper. Find one transportation word and one building word. You have two minutes.

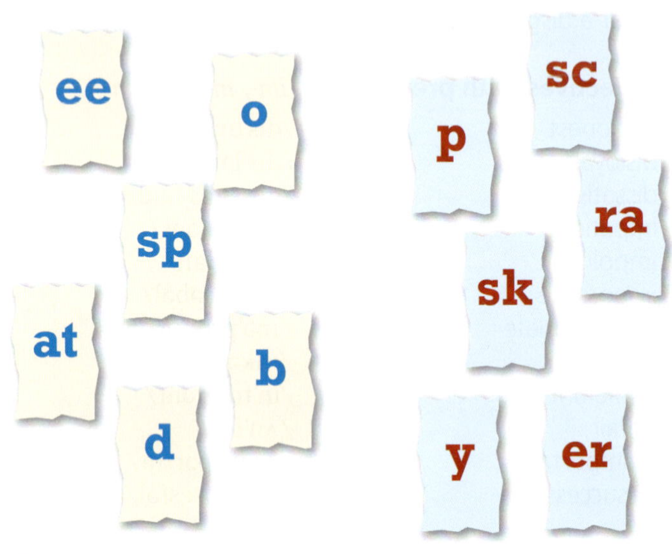

2a Find eight compound nouns. You have one minute.

snowmobile

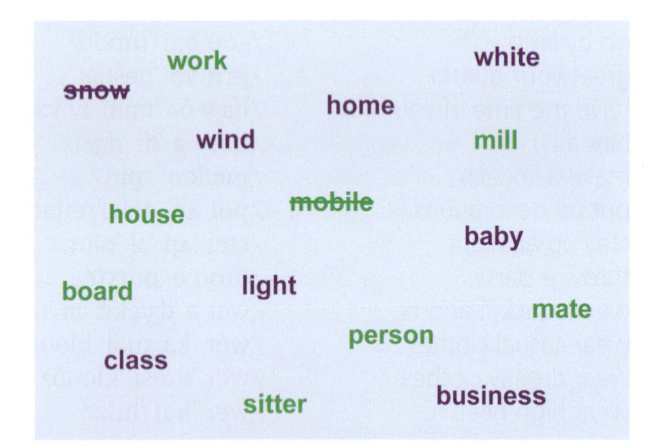

2b Arrange the letters below to make a job word and a transportation word.

3 Work in pairs. Student A acts out a phrasal verb. Student B guesses the phrase. Switch roles.

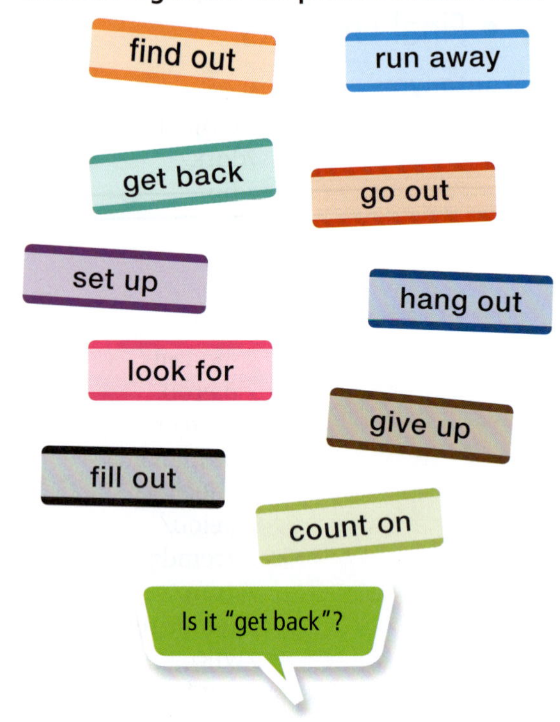

Unit 2

1 Choose a straight or diagonal line on the grid. Use the words and pictures to make up a story about something you want to do.

Brain Trainers

2 Look at the word webs for one minute. Cover them. Now write four phrases for each word web in your notebook.

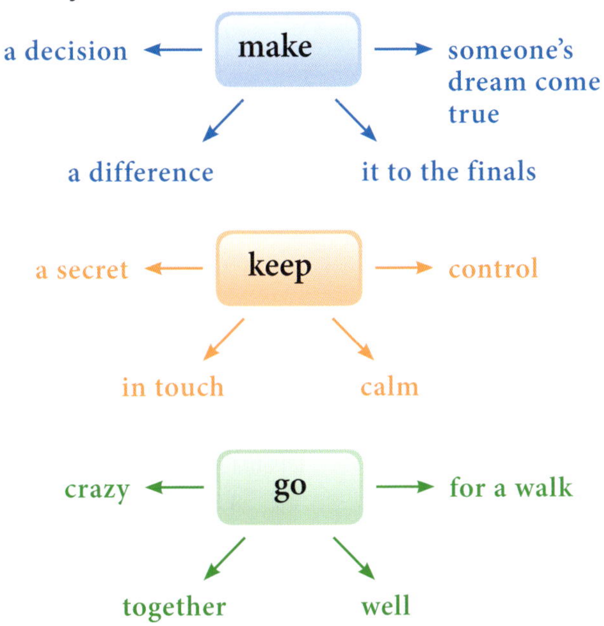

3 Work in pairs. Identify a picture. Your partner identifies the matching word.

	1	2	3	4
A		poet		playwright
B		sculptor	art	
C		novelist	photographer	

Unit 3

1a Look at the boy and girl. Can you find them in the crowd below? You have one minute.

1b Now work with a partner. Look at the crowd. Pick four people and take turns telling your partner how they are feeling.

2a How many feelings verbs can you think of with the letter *s*? Write them in your notebook.

2b Now can you think of these feelings verbs?

This is a three-letter word that ends in *y*.
This is a four-letter word. The third letter is *w*.
This is a five-letter word that begins with *f*.
This is a five-letter word that ends in *h*.

Brain Trainers

3 Look at the photos. Make adjectives from the nouns in the box to describe each photo.

beauty	~~danger~~	fame	health	luck
peace	poison	success	wealth	

1 *dangerous*

Unit 4

1 Look at the pieces of paper. Find two natural disaster words. You have two minutes.

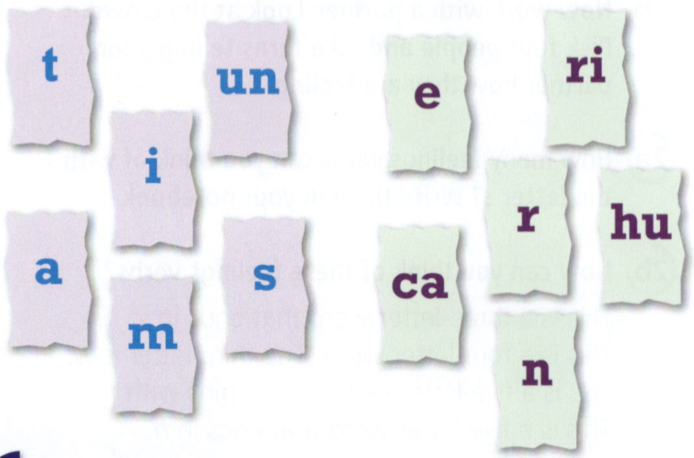

2 Work in pairs. Choose a noun from box 1. Your partner describes a natural disaster using a verb from box 2.

1	2
flood	starve
volcano	destroy
drought	erupt
famine	drown
avalanche	spread
disease	survive
earthquake	bury

flood

People can drown in a flood.

3a Work in pairs. Say a word from the list below. Your partner completes the phrasal verb. Write it in your notebook. Then switch roles. Check your answers.

take ...
keep ...
run ...
calm ...
come ...
break ...
look forward ...
figure ...
get ...
put ...

3b Now choose a phrasal verb from your list. Your partner makes a sentence using the phrasal verb. Switch roles.

Brain Trainers

Unit 5

1 Choose three objects from the grid in a straight or diagonal line. Write a story in your notebook about what happened yesterday.

2 Read the words aloud three times. Try to remember them in order. Then cover the list and write the words in your notebook. How many can you remember?

front desk	phone	inquiry
appointment	meeting	presentation

spreadsheet	office supplies	making copies
email	report	payment

3 Make eight job qualities from the letters below. You have two minutes.

tie	nt	pa		
re	le	ab	li	
tu	pu	al	nc	
te	ac	cu	ra	
al	ic	an	al	yt
ga	ed	niz	or	
en	pe	ex	ced	ri
pr	al	tic	ac	

patient

Unit 6

1a Look at the puzzle. Can you find one picture that doesn't appear twice? Look, but don't mark the puzzle. You have one minute.

1b Look at the puzzle again. Find two things to eat and two means of transportation you can find at the coast.

2 How many coast words can you make in one minute? Write them in your notebook. Use the cues to help you.

c____
p___
h___ d__ s___
s______
s__w___
cliffs

s______ s___
a________
h______
b____ u______
i__ c_____ s____

Brain Trainers

3a Read the words in the box aloud three times. Cover the box and read the list below. Which word is missing?

restore	remove	recover	research	release

3b Now try again.

disappear → discover → discontinue → dislike → disagree

discontinue	disagree	disappear	discover

Unit 7

1 Look at the pieces of paper. Find two adjectives with opposite meanings. You have two minutes.

2a Work in pairs. Choose an adjective from the list. Act it out. Your partner guesses the adjective and then says its opposite.

2b Find two more pairs of adjective opposites in the reverse spiral puzzle.

3 Look at the objects in the grid for one minute. Cover the grid and write the words in your notebook. How many can you remember?

Brain Trainers

Unit 8

1 You are a detective. Choose three objects from the grid in a straight or diagonal line. Write a story in your notebook about a crime you have solved.

2 Make eight spy phrases using all the words in the grid. Then make your own puzzle. Swap it with your partner and complete his/her puzzle.

letl	nowd	onseome	ecdode	a
pys	a	amek	no	letl
ractk	digsisue	owemhsere	ile	reaw
a	epasce	a	sgaemes	lead
morf	a	rutht	noprse	het

tell a lie

3 Work in pairs. Choose one of the boxes below. Read the words aloud three times. Cover them and write the opposites in your notebook, using *dis-*, *im-*, *in-* or *un-*. Who has the most words?

incorrect

correct	fair	honest
polite	tolerant	satisfied

appropriate	important	loyal
patient	possible	successful

Unit 9

1a Look at the boy and girl. Can you find them in the party? You have one minute.

1b Now describe what the boy and girl are wearing.

2 Work in small groups. You are planning a party. Choose a word and make a sentence about how you are going to celebrate. The next person chooses a new word and makes a new sentence. How many sentences can you make in two minutes?

Let's throw a party on Saturday night.

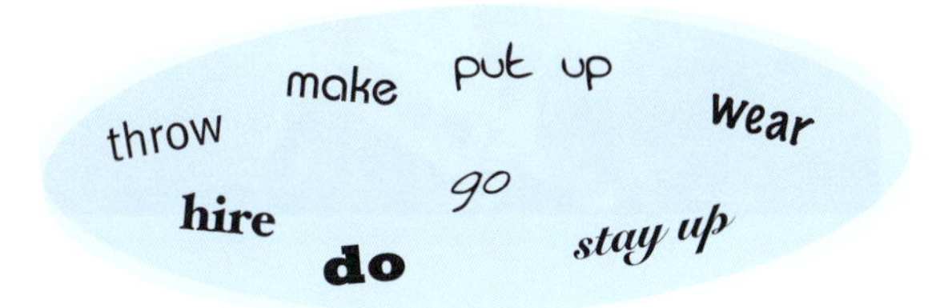

3 How many reporting verbs can you make using these letters? You can use the letters more than once. You have three minutes.

explained

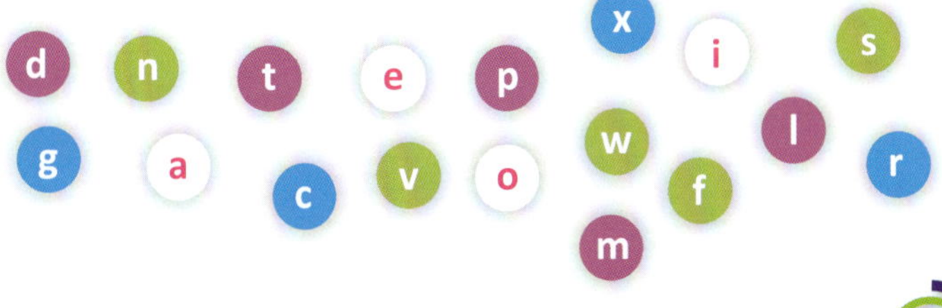

Listening Bank

Unit 1

1 **Listen again. Choose the correct options.**

1.11

1 Laura was *11* / *15* when her life changed.
2 She was *going to school* / *going home*.
3 She was thinking about *music* / *homework*.
4 The band was playing *on the street* / *in the bookstore*.
5 She *loved* / *hated* the band's music.

2 **Listen again. Are these statements true (T) or false (F)?**

1.11

1 Laura is now a famous trumpet player. *T*
2 She was excited to hear the band because they were famous.
3 There were two trumpet players, a singer and a guitar player in the band.
4 After the band finished playing, she went home.
5 When Laura asked her mom for trumpet lessons, she immediately said yes.

Unit 2

1 **Listen again. Choose the correct options.**

1.24

1 Raj has *never* / *often* sung in public.
2 His rap is about *biology class* / *school lunches*.
3 *He* / *His sister* designed the burger costume for the video.
4 *He* / *His sister* plays the guitar and drums on the video.
5 Jennifer Marquez *posted a link to* / *wrote a review of* Raj's video on her blog.
6 *Jennifer Marquez* / *Larry Nixon* has invited Raj to come to New York.

2 **Listen again. Answer the questions.**

1.24

1 How old is Raj Patel? *14*
2 How many hits did his video get?
3 What does Raj do on the video?
4 Where will Raj perform the rap?
5 How does he feel about this?

Unit 3

1 **Listen again. Choose the correct options.**

1.35

1 Luke started *acting* / *being in movies* when he was five.
2 He was *glad* / *sad* when he didn't get a movie part.
3 Now he is *happy* / *sad* that he wasn't a famous child actor.
4 He thinks that famous child actors have a *crazy* / *amazing* kind of life.
5 It *is* / *isn't* easy for child stars to become successful actors as adults.
6 He *feels* / *doesn't feel* confident about his future.

2 **Listen again. Answer the questions.**

1.35

1 What did Luke do in school?
He was in school plays.
2 Why is it hard for famous child actors to have normal friends?
3 What kind of people follow child actors?
4 Why is Luke famous now?
5 How old is he now?

Listening Bank

Unit 4

1 Listen again. Choose the correct options.
2.10
1 Mike thinks the participants in survival shows do *crazy* / *smart* things.
2 Some participants *eat things* / *interview people* that might give them a disease.
3 It *is* / *isn't* safe to swim across ice-cold rivers.
4 Mike talks about a man who *died* / *was rescued* last year.
5 It was *winter* / *summer* when this man was in the mountains.
6 Mike thinks that this person was *brave* / *stupid*.
7 In emergency situations, you *should* / *shouldn't* sleep in a snow cave.

2 Listen again. Answer the questions.
2.10
1 When is it OK to do the dangerous things seen on survival shows? *in an emergency*
2 What did the man in the mountains want to do?
3 What gave him this idea?
4 Why was he lucky?

Unit 5

1 Listen again. Choose the correct options.
2.23
1 Tom's training session starts in *10* / *30* minutes.
2 Tom is scared of *heights* / *flights*.
3 Tom is *usually* / *never* late.
4 Tom is picking up his costume *this afternoon* / *tomorrow*.
5 Anna is going to bring her *pirate costume* / *camera* when she visits the theme park.

2 Listen again. Are these statements true (T) or false (F)?
2.23
1 Tom and Anna have arranged to meet at the theme park. *F*
2 Tom doesn't like theme parks.
3 Tom starts his job today.
4 Anna is surprised that Tom has a job at the theme park.
5 Anna doesn't think that Tom is good at working with other people.
6 Tom is going to wear unusual clothes for his job.
7 Anna takes a photo of Tom.

Unit 6

1 Listen again. Put these events in the correct order.
2.36
a It was used as a school for sailors.
b The *Cutty Sark* was built. *1*
c It was damaged in a fire.
d It came in second in a famous race.
e It was moved to Greenwich.

2 Listen again. Complete the fact sheet.
2.36

CUTTY SARK FACT FILE

1 *Cutty Sark* was built in 1869 in *Scotland*.
2 It transported tea from .... to England.
3 In .... it was bought by Captain Dowman.
4 In .... it was moved to Greenwich and became a .... .
5 In 2007 it was badly damaged in a .... .
6 The repairs took five years to complete and cost over .... .
7 The ship is now raised .... meters above the ground.

Listening Bank

Unit 7

1 3.9 **Listen again and match the speakers (A–C) to the ideas (1–7). There is one idea you don't need.**

1 There'll be farms on the colony. *A*
2 There'll be one home at first and another one many years later.
3 The colony will be completely dark.
4 People will eat plants from the ocean.
5 It will be possible to play soccer and go shopping.
6 There will be more than 1,000 colonists.
7 The colony won't be in deep water.

2 3.9 **Listen again. Complete the sentences.**

1 According to speaker A, the boats for the floating cities will be much *bigger* than ordinary boats.
2 Speaker B thinks that there will be colonies on the ocean floor in .... years.
3 Speaker C talks about going to a planet outside our .... .
4 The planet would have .... and air that we could breathe.
5 The journey to this planet might take .... years.

Unit 8

1 3.22 **Listen again. Complete the sentences with *David, Eleanor, Eric* or *Anna*.**

1 *Eric*'s phone was stolen.
2 .... already has some experience of CCTV cameras.
3 .... thinks that cameras are a good idea.
4 .... is angry because the school didn't tell the students about the cameras.
5 .... thinks that cameras are unimportant.
6 .... thinks that classes might be more boring with CCTV cameras.

2 3.22 **Listen again. Choose the correct options.**

1 David felt *uncomfortable* / *dissatisfied* about the cameras at first.
2 Eleanor found out about the cameras *yesterday* / *this morning*.
3 Eleanor thinks that the situation is *inappropriate* / *unfair*.
4 Eric thinks that if there had been cameras in the *hallways* / *classrooms*, they would have found the thief.
5 Anna's teachers are usually *relaxed* / *angry*.

Unit 9

1 3.34 **Listen again. Are these statements true (T) or false (F)?**

1 People of all ages have a public holiday in Japan today. *T*
2 There's a celebration for everyone who has his/her birthday on this day.
3 Azumi often wears these clothes.
4 She asked her grandmother for advice about the clothes.
5 Azumi's parents made a speech at the ceremony.
6 Azumi and her friends are going to a party.

2 3.34 **Listen again. Complete the sentences.**

1 The day is called "*Coming-of-Age* Day."
2 Azumi's *furisode* is long, warm and .... .
3 She has .... the dress for the day.
4 The ceremony was at the city government .... .
5 At the party, they're going to .... .

Pronunciation

Unit 1 • Compound noun word stress

a 1.4 **Listen and repeat. Then mark the stressed syllables.**

babysitter firefighter homework speedboat

b 1.4 **Listen, check your answers and repeat.**

Unit 2 • Sentence stress

a 1.18 **Listen and repeat.**

1 Don't forget to keep in touch when you move.
2 I made a bad decision when I sold my bike.
3 Please try to keep control of your dog!

b 1.18 **Listen again and find the stressed words.**

Unit 3 • Showing feelings

a 1.29 **Listen and decide how each speaker is feeling. Write *a* for speaker one or *b* for speaker two.**

1 What's that?	angry *b*	afraid *a*
2 It's great news!	excited	bored ....
3 Look! A shark!	afraid	excited ....

b 1.29 **Listen again and repeat.**

Unit 4 • Consonant clusters

a 2.3 **Listen and repeat.**

<u>spr</u>ead eru<u>pt</u> de<u>str</u>oy

b 2.4 **Listen and repeat.**

1 The volcano erupted on Wednesday.
2 Don't scream so loudly! It's just a squirrel.
3 Stop spreading crazy stories.

Unit 5 • /ɚ/ and /ɔr/

a 2.15 **Listen and repeat.**

/ɚ/ work /ɔr/ report

b 2.16 **Match these words to the correct sound (/ɚ/ or /ɔr/). Then listen and check.**

bird door heard order serve sport

Unit 6 • Weak vs strong form of *was*

a 2.30 **Listen to the conversation. Underline the weak pronunciation of *was* /wəz/.**

A Was there a beach festival here last year?
B Yes, there **was**. And a movie **was** made about it.
C It **was** directed by Felipe Trent.
B Was it really?
C Yes, it **was**. And it **was** shown on TV last night.

b 2.30 **Listen again and repeat. Practice the conversation in groups of three.**

Unit 7 • Elided syllables

a 3.2 **Listen and repeat. How many syllables can you hear in each word? Which letters aren't spoken?**

Wednesday camera comfortable

b 3.3 **Listen and repeat. Find the letters that aren't spoken in the underlined words.**

1 It's a <u>different</u> <u>temperature</u> today.
2 Do you prefer <u>chocolate</u> or <u>vegetables</u>?
3 They have some <u>interesting</u> <u>local</u> dishes here.

Unit 8 • /ɛr/, /i/ and /eɪ/

a 3.15 **Listen and repeat.**

/ɛr/ wear /i/ deal /eɪ/ break

b 3.16 **Match these words to the correct sound (/ɛr/, /i/ or /eɪ/). Then listen and check.**

air chair escape heat police take

Unit 9 • /ʃ/, /ʒ/ and /dʒ/

a 3.27 **Listen and repeat.**

/ʃ/ decorations /ʒ/ casual /dʒ/ jacket

b 3.28 **Listen and repeat.**

1 She's studying geography in college.
2 I usually do martial arts in my pajamas.
3 The electrician left some trash in the garage.
4 He just watches action movies on television.

Culture 1 Halloween

Reading

1 Read about Halloween. Name four countries where Halloween is celebrated.
3.39

2 Read about Halloween again. Answer the questions.

1 Why did people wear costumes on Halloween in the past?
2 Why do people sometimes throw eggs on Halloween?
3 Why do people put pumpkins outside their home?
4 Why is it lucky to find a ring in your cake on Halloween?

Your Culture

3 In pairs, answer the questions.

1 Do people in your country celebrate Halloween or All Saints' Day? What do they do?
2 Are there other festivals in which people wear costumes? Describe them.
3 Barmbrack has a ring inside it. Are there any traditions in your country in which people put objects or symbols inside food?

4 Write a short paragraph about Halloween in your country. Use your answers to Exercise 3 and the Halloween examples to help you.

HALLOWEEN

October 31 is Halloween, the night before All Saints' Day. In many parts of the world, it's the scariest night of the year!

Costumes in the past
People in Britain and Ireland used to believe that when people died, their souls stayed on earth until All Saints' Day. Halloween was the last time that these souls could get revenge on their enemies. For this reason, people wore costumes and masks so the souls couldn't recognize them.

Costumes today
Many people still wear costumes on Halloween today. In the UK, children usually dress as scary characters, like witches, zombies or vampires. In the US and Canada, a wider variety of costumes are worn, and there are a lot of costume parties for adults as well as children.

Trick-or-treaters
In their costumes, children go to people's homes and say "Trick or treat?" People usually give the children a treat—for example, some candy. If the children aren't given anything, they can sometimes play a trick on the people. For example, they might throw an egg at the front door.

Pumpkins
People cut a scary face into a pumpkin and light a candle inside it. They put this outside their house as a sign that they have treats for the trick-or-treaters.

Barmbrack
In Ireland, people eat a traditional fruitcake called "barmbrack" on Halloween. Inside the cake, there's a ring. The person with the ring in his or her piece of cake will find true love in the next year.

Culture 2 New Year's Eve

Reading

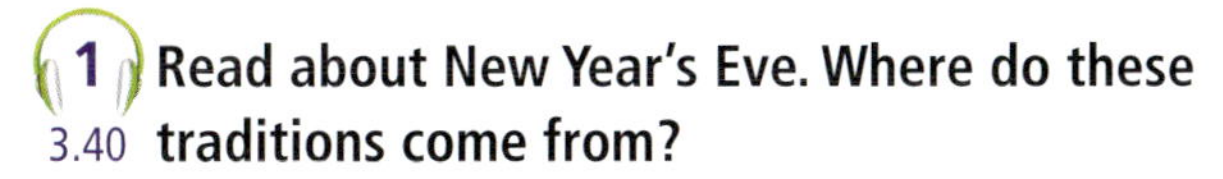

1 3.40 **Read about New Year's Eve. Where do these traditions come from?**

first-footing	a cake	beach parties
a ball of lights	a song about old friends	

2 **Read about New Year's Eve again. Answer the questions.**

1 What is Hogmanay?
2 What happens on Sydney Harbor Bridge?
3 What do people do when they sing *Auld Lang Syne*?
4 What is a New Year's Resolution?

Your Culture

3 **In pairs, answer the questions.**

1 Do people in your country celebrate New Year's Eve? How?
2 Do they have special food or drink on that night?
3 *Auld Lang Syne* is a traditional song for New Year's Eve. What traditional songs are associated with festivals in your country?

4 **Write a short paragraph about New Year's Eve in your country. Use your answers to Exercise 3 and the New Year's Eve examples to help you.**

At midnight on December 31, we say goodbye to the old year and welcome the new one. Here are some of the traditions around the world.

Hogmanay

This is the Scottish word for New Year, and it's a very important celebration in Scotland. After midnight, people go "first-footing." This means being the first person of the year to enter someone else's home. It brings good luck to the household. First-footers are usually given food and drink, but they can also bring a cake as a gift for the homeowner and his or her family.

Times Square

About a million people go to Times Square in New York on New Year's Eve. A big ball of lights drops slowly down a flagpole. When it reaches the bottom, the new year has begun!

New Year on the beach

In Australia, New Year's Eve is in summer. Most Australians celebrate outside—on boats, in parks or at the beach.
In Sydney, there is a parade of boats in the harbor, and at midnight, there is a spectacular fireworks display on Sydney Harbor Bridge.

Auld Lang Syne

This is a traditional Scottish song about remembering old friends. It is sung in many parts of the world at midnight on New Year's Eve. To sing the song, people stand in a circle, cross their arms and hold hands.

New Year's Resolutions

On New Year's Day, a lot of people decide to stop a bad habit or start a good one. This decision is called a "New Year's Resolution." More people exercise in January than in any other month. Unfortunately, most resolutions are forgotten by the beginning of February!

Culture  Chinese New Year

Reading

1 3.41 **Read about Chinese New Year. Put these Chinese New Year traditions in the correct order.**

a big meal	cleaning the house
dragon dances	painting the house door red

2 Read about Chinese New Year again. Answer the questions.

1 Why are Chinese New Year decorations often red?
2 How long is the vacation that people have at New Year in China?
3 Why are red envelopes important at New Year?
4 Why do people go to Chinatown in Sydney at Chinese New Year?

Your Culture

3 In pairs, answer the questions.

1 Are there any Chinese New Year celebrations in your country? What happens at them?
2 Are there any other important festivals from other cultures that are celebrated in your country? Which?
3 Fireworks are an important part of Chinese New Year. Do you have fireworks in your country? When?

4 Write a short paragraph about Chinese New Year or another festival celebrated in your country. Use your answers to Exercise 3 and the Chinese New Year examples to help you.

CHINESE NEW YEAR

New Year is the longest and most important festival in China, but it isn't celebrated on January 1. It is on a different date each year, between January 21 and February 20.

Preparations

The whole house is cleaned before the festival to sweep away the bad luck of the previous year. Red is a lucky color in China, so people often put up red decorations or paint their doors red. The house is now ready to welcome the good luck of the New Year.

Reunion dinner

Many people in China live a long way from their family, but everyone can go home at New Year because there are seven days of vacation. On the night before New Year, there is a special meal for the whole family.

New Year's Day

There are fireworks to drive away evil spirits. There are lion and dragon dances, too. Parents and grandparents give children money in red envelopes.

Chinese New Year around the world

Chinese New Year is an important festival in every place where large groups of Chinese people are living. It is a public holiday in Malaysia, Singapore, Mauritius, Indonesia and the Philippines. There are parades in many cities, including San Francisco and Los Angeles (US), London (UK), Toronto (Canada) and Wellington (New Zealand). The biggest celebration outside Asia, however, is in Sydney (Australia). More than 600,000 people go to the city's Chinatown every year to enjoy Chinese food, parades, dragon boat races and performances from some of Asia's best singers and dancers.

Culture  Valentine's Day

Reading

1 (3.42) **Read about Valentine's Day. What different things do people give to each other?**

2 **Read about Valentine's Day again. Answer the questions.**

1 What romantic thing did the priest Valentine do?
2 When did Valentine's Day start to be a celebration of love?
3 If you like getting cards on Valentine's Day, what job should you have?
4 What is White Day?

Your Culture

3 **In pairs, answer the questions.**

1 Do people in your country celebrate Valentine's Day? What do they do?
2 Are candies or chocolates part of the tradition on Valentine's Day? Are they important on any other holiday?
3 Are any other saints' days celebrated in your country? How?

4 **Write a short paragraph about Valentine's Day in your country. Use your answers to Exercise 3 and the Valentine's Day examples to help you.**

Valentine's Day

Valentine's Day (or Saint Valentine's Day) is celebrated on February 14, and it's a celebration of love in many parts of the world.

Early in the history of Christianity, three saints named Valentine were killed for their religion. They didn't do anything very romantic, but stories were written about one of these Valentines long after his death. He was a priest in Rome, and in the stories, he helped a lot of young couples to get married in secret. They couldn't marry publicly because the Roman emperor at the time wanted men to be soldiers, not husbands.

Valentine's Day started to be a day for romance in the Middle Ages, and by the nineteenth century, people were sending romantic cards and gifts to the person they loved. The cards were called "valentines," and the tradition of sending them continues in most English-speaking countries today. People don't usually write their name on the card so their identity is a secret.

Some people also give flowers, heart-shaped chocolates and other presents to their boyfriend or girlfriend. In the evening, restaurants are full of romantic couples. In the US, about a billion valentines are given every year. Younger children often give cards to all their family and friends, and the people who receive the most valentines are usually teachers.

Valentine's Day is also an important day in Japan and Korea. Women buy men chocolates on February 14. This is followed by White Day on March 14, when men buy women candy. Half of all the chocolate in Japan is bought for Valentine's Day!

Culture  Saint Patrick's Day

Reading

1 3.43 **Read about St. Patrick's Day. Name nine countries that celebrate St. Patrick's Day.**

2 Read about St. Patrick's Day again. Answer the questions.

1 St. Patrick went to Ireland twice. Why did he go there the first time? And the second?
2 Why is Downpatrick an important place on St. Patrick's Day?
3 What happens in Chicago on St. Patrick's Day?
4 Where is the world's biggest St. Patrick's Day parade?

Your Culture

3 In pairs, answer the questions.

1 Which famous people from history does your country or area celebrate?
2 Are there public holidays for the celebrations?
3 How do people celebrate?

4 Write a short paragraph about St. Patrick's Day or another day celebrated in your country. Use your answers to Exercise 3 and the St. Patrick's Day examples to help you.

St. Patrick's Day

St. Patrick

Born: around AD 400, in Britain

Life: Some pirates caught him when he was sixteen and sold him as a slave in Ireland. After six years, he escaped and went to France to study religion. Later he traveled around Ireland for many years, talking to people about Christianity.

Symbol: the shamrock

St. Patrick's Day falls on March 17, and it's an important date in Ireland. It's also celebrated in other parts of the world where Irish people have gone to live.

In Ireland

St. Patrick's Day is a public holiday. People wear green clothes and shamrocks, and there are parades and parties. The biggest parades are in Ireland's capital city, Dublin, and in Downpatrick in Northern Ireland because people think St. Patrick died there. There are also a lot of important traditional Irish sports games that day.

In the US

In the past, a lot of Irish people immigrated to the US, and St. Patrick's Day is important there for both Irish and non-Irish people. In Chicago and other cities, they put green dye in the river on St. Patrick's Day. There are parades, too. The parade in New York is the biggest in the world. Usually about 150,000 people march in the parade, and two million people stand in the streets to watch.

Around the world

St. Patrick's Day is a public holiday in some parts of Canada and on the Caribbean island of Montserrat. There are parades in Britain, Korea and Japan, and street parties in New Zealand and Argentina.

Culture 6 May Day

Reading

1 (3.44) **Read about May Day. How many different names for May Day are mentioned?**

2 Read about May Day again. Answer the questions.

1 Why are ribbons important on May Day?
2 What do the people of Padstow do on May 1?
3 Why was 1994 an important year in the history of South Africa?
4 What must the Lei Queen be good at?

Your Culture

3 In pairs, answer the questions.

1 Is May 1 a holiday in your country? How is it celebrated?
2 Are there any holidays with special dances in your country? Describe the dances.
3 Think of a town or city in your area that is famous for an unusual holiday. Describe the celebration.

4 Write a short paragraph about May Day in your country. Use your answers to Exercise 3 and the May Day examples to help you.

Maypole Dance

Padstow

Lei Queen

MAY DAY

May Day is May 1—or sometimes the first Monday in May—and has important traditions in many English-speaking countries.

Maypole Dance

A Maypole is a tall pole, and the traditional May Day dance in England and the US is danced around it. Each dancer holds the end of a ribbon. The other end of the ribbon is attached to the top of the Maypole. The dancers make a pretty pattern with the ribbons.

Padstow

Padstow, a small town in southwestern England, is famous for its celebrations on May 1. There are usually crowds of about 30,000 people. Flags and flowers decorate the streets, and two people in strange black costumes dance through the town. All the townspeople wear white clothes and sing and dance behind them.

Labor Day

Around the world, May 1 is a day to celebrate the rights of working people. There are a lot of protests and marches. In South Africa, May 1 was once marked by protests against unfair laws aimed at black people. The laws changed in 1994, and since then the day has been an important public holiday.

Lei Day

In Hawaii, May Day is Lei Day. A "lei" is a traditional necklace of flowers worn in Hawaii, and Lei Day is a celebration of Hawaiian culture. There are contests in hula dancing and lei making, and a Lei Queen is chosen for her skills in these activities.

Irregular Verb List

Verb	Past Simple	Past Participle
be	was/were	been
become	became	become
begin	began	begun
break	broke	broken
bring	brought	brought
build	built	built
buy	bought	bought
can	could	been able
catch	caught	caught
choose	chose	chosen
come	came	come
cost	cost	cost
cut	cut	cut
do	did	done
draw	drew	drawn
drink	drank	drunk
drive	drove	driven
eat	ate	eaten
fall	fell	fallen
feed	fed	fed
feel	felt	felt
fight	fought	fought
find	found	found
fly	flew	flown
forget	forgot	forgotten
get	got	gotten
give	gave	given
go	went	gone/been
grow	grew	grown
have	had	had
hear	heard	heard
hold	held	held
keep	kept	kept
know	knew	known
leave	left	left
lend	lent	lent

Verb	Past Simple	Past Participle
light	lit	lit
lose	lost	lost
make	made	made
mean	meant	meant
meet	met	met
pay	paid	paid
put	put	put
read /rid/	read /rɛd/	read /rɛd/
ride	rode	ridden
ring	rang	rung
run	ran	run
say	said	said
see	saw	seen
sell	sold	sold
send	sent	sent
shine	shone	shone
show	showed	shown
sing	sang	sung
sit	sat	sat
sleep	slept	slept
speak	spoke	spoken
spend	spent	spent
stand	stood	stood
steal	stole	stolen
swim	swam	swum
take	took	taken
teach	taught	taught
tell	told	told
think	thought	thought
throw	threw	thrown
understand	understood	understood
wake	woke	woken
wear	wore	worn
win	won	won
write	wrote	written